EFFECTIVE
SUPERVISION

ASCD MEMBER BOOK

Many ASCD members received this book as a
member benefit upon its initial release.

Learn more at: **www.ascd.org/memberbooks**

EFFECTIVE SUPERVISION

SUPPORTING THE ART AND SCIENCE OF TEACHING

ROBERT J. **MARZANO**

TONY **FRONTIER**

DAVID **LIVINGSTON**

ASCD

Alexandria, Virginia USA

ASCD

1703 N. Beauregard St. • Alexandria, VA 22311-1714 USA
Phone: 800-933-2723 or 703-578-9600 • Fax: 703-575-5400
Website: www.ascd.org • E-mail: member@ascd.org
Author guidelines: www.ascd.org/write

Gene R. Carter, *Executive Director;* Judy Zimny, *Chief Program Development Officer,* Nancy Modrak, *Publisher;* Scott Willis, *Director, Book Acquisitions & Development;* Julie Houtz, *Director, Book Editing & Production;* Deborah Siegel, *Editor;* Greer Wymond, *Senior Graphic Designer;* Mike Kalyan, *Production Manager;* Keith Demmons, *Desktop Publishing Specialist*

All web links in this book are correct as of the publication date below but may have become inactive or otherwise modified since that time. If you notice a deactivated or changed link, please e-mail books@ascd. org with the words "Link Update" in the subject line. In your message, please specify the web link, the book title, and the page number on which the link appears.

ASCD Member Book, No. FY11-7 (May 2011, P). ASCD Member Books mail to Premium (P), Select (S), and Institutional Plus (I+) members on this schedule: Jan., PSI+; Feb., P; Apr., PSI+; May, P; July, PSI+; Aug., P; Sept., PSI+; Nov., PSI+; Dec., P. Select membership was formerly known as Comprehensive membership.

PAPERBACK ISBN: 978-1-4166-1155-4 ASCD product # 110019
Also available as an e-book (see Books in Print for the ISBNs).

Quantity discounts for the paperback edition only: 10–49 copies, 10%; 50+ copies, 15%; for 1,000 or more copies, call 800-933-2723, ext. 5634, or 703-575-5634. For desk copies: member@ascd.org.

Library of Congress Cataloging-in-Publication Data

Marzano, Robert J.
  Effective supervision : supporting the art and science of teaching / Robert J. Marzano, Tony Frontier, David Livingston.
      p. cm.
  Includes bibliographical references and index.
  ISBN 978-1-4166-1155-4 (pbk. : alk. paper) 1. School supervision. 2. Teachers–In-service training. 3. Performance standards. I. Frontier, Tony. II. Livingston, David. III. Title.
  LB2838.M3768 2011
  371.2'03–dc22
                              2010053867

20 19 18 17 16 15 14 13 12 11   1 2 3 4 5 6 7 8 9 10

EFFECTIVE SUPERVISION

SUPPORTING THE ART AND SCIENCE OF TEACHING

CHAPTER 1

Supervision That Develops Expertise

Supervision has been a central feature on the landscape of K–12 education almost from the outset of schooling in this country. Witness the following comments from a 1709 document entitled "Reports of the Record of Commissions of the City of Boston" (cited in Burke & Krey, 2005, p. 411):

> [It should] be therefore established a committee of inspectors to visit ye School from time to time, when as oft as they shall see fit, to Enform themselves of the methods used in teacher of ye Scholars and Inquire of their proficiency, and be present at the performance of some of their Exercises.

In the three centuries that have transpired since this proclamation of 1709, the world of K–12 education has changed dramatically. Along with changes in curriculum, instruction, and assessment have come changes in perspectives on supervision and evaluation. In Chapter 2, we briefly trace these changes to provide a frame of reference for the recommendations made in this book. Throughout the remainder of the book, we lay out a comprehensive approach to supervision as well as address the implications of our approach for the practice of evaluation.

The Foundational Principle of Supervision

The recommendations in this book are grounded in one primary principle that we view as foundational to the evolution of supervision: **the purpose of supervision should be the enhancement of teachers' pedagogical skills, with the ultimate goal of enhancing student achievement.** Even a brief examination of the research attests to the logic underlying this principle. Specifically, one incontestable fact in the research on schooling is that student achievement in classes with highly skilled teachers is better than student achievement in classes with less skilled teachers. To determine just how much better, consider Figure 1.1.

| FIGURE 1.1 | Teacher Expertise and Student Achievement |

Teacher Skill Percentile Rank	Predicted Percentile Gain for Student at the 50th Percentile	Predicted Percentile Rank for Student
50th	0	50th
70th	8	58th
90th	18	68th
98th	27	77th

Note: For a discussion of how these figures were computed, see Marzano and Waters (2009).

Figure 1.1 depicts the expected percentile gain in achievement for a student starting at the 50th percentile within classrooms taught by teachers of varying degrees of competence. A student at the 50th percentile will not be expected to gain at all in percentile rank in the classroom of a teacher of the 50th percentile in terms of his or her pedagogical skill. However, a student at the 50th percentile will be expected to advance to the 58th percentile in the class of a teacher at the 70th percentile in terms of pedagogical skill. The increase in student percentile rank is even larger in the classrooms of teachers at the 90th and 98th percentile ranks in terms of their pedagogical skill. Students in these situations would be expected to reach the 68th and 77th percentiles, respectively. Clearly, the more skilled the teacher, the greater the predicted increase in student achievement. Equally clear is the implication for supervision. Its primary purpose should be the enhancement of teacher expertise.

Although it is unreasonable to expect all teachers to reach the lofty status of the 90th percentile or higher regarding their pedagogical skills, it is reasonable to expect all teachers to increase their expertise from year to year. Even a modest increase would yield impressive results. Specifically, if a teacher at the 50th percentile in terms of his or her pedagogical skill raised his or her competence by two percentile points each year, the average achievement of his or her students would be expected to increase by eight percentile points over a 10-year period.

We believe that when done well, the process of supervision can be instrumental in producing incremental gains in teacher expertise, which can produce incremental gains in student achievement. Additionally, we believe that the research provides rather clear guidance on how to enhance teacher expertise.

The Nature of Expertise

Relatively speaking, it was not that long ago that expertise was considered something that could not be developed. Rather, expertise was thought of as a natural by-product of talent. In his review of the historical literature on perceptions of expertise, Murray (1989) concluded that it was generally believed that talent was considered "a gift from the gods." About this notion, Ericsson and Charness (1994) note:

> One important reason for this bias in attribution . . . is linked to immediate legitimization of various activities associated with the gifts. If the gods have bestowed a child with a special gift in a given art form, who would dare to oppose its development, and who would not facilitate its expression so everyone could enjoy its wonderful creations. This argument may appear strange today, but before the French Revolution the privileged status of kings and nobility and birthright of their children were primarily based on such claims. (p. 726)

Talent bestowed by the gods, then, was considered the prime determiner of expertise. Over time, the fallacies in this perspective were disclosed. Ericsson and Charness explain that "it is curious how little empirical evidence supports the talent view of expert and exceptional performance" (p. 730). They note that over the centuries, the talent hypothesis was inevitably challenged once it became evident that individuals could "dramatically increase their performance through education and training if they had the necessary drive and motivation" (p. 727).

Akin to the talent hypothesis is the intelligence hypothesis: highly intelligent people have the capacity to learn more, quicker. Over time, this trajectory leads to expertise. Ericsson, Krampe, and Tesch-Romer (1993) note that this hypothesis has little backing: "The relationship of IQ to exceptional performance is rather weak in many domains" (p. 364).

If expertise is not a function of talent or intelligence, what then *are* its determiners? Based on the research on expertise, we propose five conditions that must be met if a district or school wishes to systematically develop teacher expertise: (1) a well-articulated knowledge base for teaching, (2) focused feedback and practice, (3) opportunities to observe and discuss expertise, (4) clear criteria and a plan for success, and (5) recognition of expertise. We consider each condition briefly here and in depth in subsequent chapters. We further assert that these five elements are necessary and sufficient conditions to raise the level of teacher expertise across a district or school. Stated differently, if a district or school were to address these five elements, they would realize an increase in teacher expertise that would translate into enhanced student achievement.

A Well-Articulated Knowledge Base for Teaching

A well-articulated knowledge base is a prerequisite for developing expertise in a systematic way within any domain. Ericsson et al. (1993) note that the extant knowledge base has increased and is continuing to increase in a variety of domains. This accumulation of knowledge renders expert status more available to more people:

> As the level of performance in the domain increased in skill and complexity, methods to explicitly instruct and train individuals were developed. In all major domains there has been a steady accumulation of knowledge about the best methods to attain a high level of performance and the associated practice activities leading to this performance. (p. 368)

As is the case with most fields of study, education has experienced exponential growth in its knowledge base, particularly regarding effective pedagogy. There have been many attempts to codify this knowledge base (see Hattie, 1992; Hattie, Biggs, & Purdie, 1996; and Wang, Haertel, & Walberg, 1993). We have organized that knowledge base into four related domains:

Domain 1: Classroom Strategies and Behaviors

Domain 2: Planning and Preparing

Domain 3: Reflecting on Teaching

Domain 4: Collegiality and Professionalism

These domains bear a resemblance to the very popular model of teaching proposed by Charlotte Danielson (1996, 2007). Her model includes the following domains:

Domain 1: Planning and Preparation

Domain 2: The Classroom Environment

Domain 3: Instruction

Domain 4: Professional Responsibilities

Although our domains bear some resemblance to Danielson's, there are significant differences in the assumed relationship between domains and the specifics within the domains. Danielson explains that her domains "are not the only possible description of practice" (p. 1). The same holds true for our model. That noted, we propose that our four domains not only represent a viable way to organize the research and theory on teaching, but also disclose some important causal linkages (see Figure 1.2).

| FIGURE 1.2 | Relationship Among Domains |

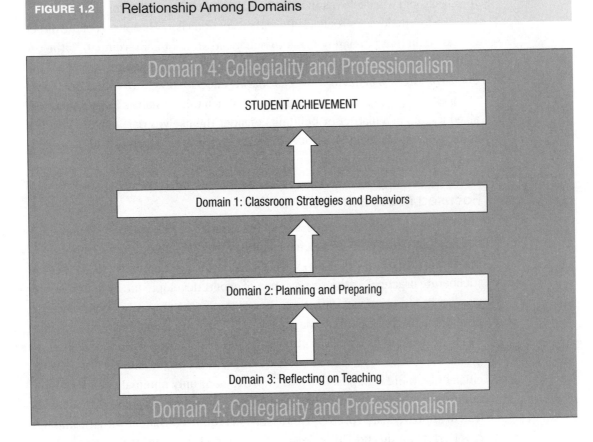

Figure 1.2 indicates that classroom strategies and behaviors (Domain 1) are at the top of the sequence and have a direct effect on student achievement. Stated differently, what occurs in the classroom has the most direct causal link to student achievement.

Directly below classroom strategies and behaviors is planning and preparing (Domain 2). As the name implies, this domain addresses the manner in which—and the extent to which—teachers prepare themselves for their day-to-day classroom work by organizing the content within lessons and the lessons within units.

Directly below planning and preparing is Domain 3—reflecting on teaching. By definition, most of the elements in this domain are evaluative in nature, in that teachers are considering their areas of strength and weakness with the overall goal of improvement. This domain has a direct link to planning and preparing. Teachers will probably improve very little in their ability to plan and prepare without carefully reflecting on their strengths and weaknesses. Without growth in planning and preparing, teachers will experience little growth in the classroom strategies and behaviors they employ. Finally, little change in what teachers do in the classroom will likely result in little change in student achievement.

The fourth domain—collegiality and professionalism—is not part of the direct causal chain that ultimately leads to enhanced student achievement. Rather, it represents the professional culture in which the other domains operate. This domain addresses behaviors such as sharing effective practices with other teachers, mentoring other teachers, and the like. When this domain is functioning well, all educators in a district or building consider themselves part of a team with a collective responsibility for students' well-being and achievement. In Chapter 3, we discuss these domains in depth.

Focused Feedback and Practice

The second element necessary for a district or school to systematically develop teacher expertise is focused feedback and practice. In their comprehensive review of the research on expertise, Ericsson and Charness (1994) identify "deliberate practice" as the *sine qua non* of expert development. Deliberate practice is a broad construct with a number of important elements. As it relates to developing teacher expertise, Marzano (2010a) has noted that deliberate practice can be thought of as a multifaceted construct. One central feature of deliberate practice is feedback. As Ericsson et al. (1993) explain: "In the absence of feedback, efficient learning is impossible and improvement only minimal even for highly motivated subjects. Hence, mere repetition of an activity will not automatically lead to improvement" (p. 367). This assertion is quite consistent with the findings reported by Hattie and Timperley (2007) from their analysis of 12 meta-analyses incorporating 196 studies and 6,972 effect sizes. The average effect size for providing feedback was 0.79, which they note is approximately twice the average effect size (0.40) associated with most educational innovations.

For feedback to be instrumental in developing teacher expertise, it must focus on specific classroom strategies and behaviors (Domain 1) during a set interval of time. For example, a given teacher might focus on specific strategies or behaviors from Domain 1 throughout a given quarter or semester. The feedback to that teacher during that quarter or semester would be on that specific strategy or behavior as opposed to the many other aspects of Domain 1 that could be the subject of feedback. The idea behind this degree of selectivity is that skill development requires focus. Feedback that involves too many elements or is too broad has little influence.

With focused feedback in place, teachers can engage in focused practice—another critical element of deliberate practice. Here the teacher practices the selected strategy or behavior experimenting with small variations in technique to determine what works best in his or her particular situation. We address specific approaches to focused feedback and practice in Chapter 4.

Opportunities to Observe and Discuss Expertise

One interesting aspect of expertise is that it manifests as nuanced behavior. Ambady and Rosenthal (1992, 1993) refer to this phenomenon as "thin slices of behavior." Relative to teaching, one can think of thin slices of behavior as the moment-to-moment adaptations a teacher makes regarding the use of specific strategies. Nuanced behavior, or thin slices of behavior, cannot be easily described but can be observed and analyzed. Consequently, opportunities to observe and discuss effective teaching are an important part of developing expertise among classroom teachers. If teachers do not have opportunities to observe and interact with other teachers, their method of generating new knowledge about teaching is limited to personal trial and error.

Although opportunities to observe and discuss expertise are not currently very common in K–12 schools, they are desired by teachers. In his book *A Place Called School*, which summarized data from 1,350 elementary and secondary teachers, Goodlad (1984) reported that "approximately three quarters of our sample at all levels of schooling indicated that they would like to observe other teachers at work" (p. 188). Similarly, in his article "Teacher Isolation and the New Reform," Flinders (1988) noted that although teachers work in isolation, they crave professional interaction with other teachers. This interaction involves both observing other teachers and interacting with them about teaching. Finally, the call for teachers to observe and discuss expertise is consistent with current discussions of professional learning communities (PLCs). As Louis, Kruse, and Associates (1995) note, one of the primary functions of the PLC movement is the "deprivitization" of practice.

In Chapter 5, we address ways to provide opportunities for teachers to observe and discuss expertise in depth. Briefly, though, we recommend that districts and schools provide opportunities for teachers to observe videotapes of other teachers, to observe expert teachers in their classrooms, to consult with expert teachers face-to-face, and to interact with their peers face-to-face as well as through synchronous and asynchronous technologies.

Clear Criteria and a Plan for Success

A critical aspect of deliberate practice is clear criteria for success. Quite obviously, relative to expertise in teaching, classroom strategies and behaviors (Domain 1) should include specific criteria as to what constitutes effective teaching. In Chapter 3, we describe 41 categories of classroom strategies and behaviors within Domain 1. For each of these 41 elements, scales (i.e., rubrics) are provided that describe novice-to-expert use of the element. Using these scales, teachers can track the development of their pedagogical expertise on specific elements over specific intervals of time.

It is tempting to embrace the position that teacher effectiveness regarding the strategies and behaviors in Domain 1 should be the sole measure of teacher performance. This approach would be a mistake. While the reasoned use of classroom strategies and behaviors is certainly a necessary ingredient of expertise, the ultimate criterion for expert performance in the classroom is student achievement. Anything else misses the point. This is depicted in Figure 1.2. Note that student achievement is at the top of the causal hierarchy. Stated differently, the ultimate criterion for successful teaching must be student learning.

In Chapter 6, we provide a number of ways to collect and use student achievement data as part of the criteria for successful teaching. We make the case that achievement data should be value added in nature. Value-added achievement data measure how much students have learned over a given interval of time. One type of value-added achievement data that might be used is knowledge gain. For example, the differences between pre-test and post-test scores on some common assessment or benchmark assessment would constitute a measure of knowledge gain for each student. Currently, knowledge gain is being used as a criterion for teacher evaluation in some districts. Other indices that can be used include residual scores and students' self-report of their knowledge gain.

With clear criteria in place for the classroom strategies and behaviors in Domain 1 and student value-added achievement, teachers can construct professional growth and development plans. These plans operationalize deliberate practice in that they describe how teachers will meet their goals and allow them to monitor progress toward their goals.

Recognition of Expertise

One characteristic of expertise in any field is that it takes a long time to develop. In fact, according to some researchers and theorists, it takes at least a decade—a fact that has been referred to as the "10-year rule" (Simon & Chase, 1973). Ericsson et al. (1993) have demonstrated the ubiquity of the 10-year rule. Regardless of the field, about 10 years of deliberate practice is required to reach expert status.

From the perspective of the 10-year rule, it is easy to conclude that acquiring expert status in teaching requires a high level of motivation on the part of aspirants. As Ericsson et al. (1993) explain:

> On the basis of several thousand years of education, along with more recent laboratory research on learning and skill acquisition, a number of conditions for optimal learning and improvement of performance have been uncovered. . . . The most cited condition concerns subjects' motivation to attend to the task and exert effort to improve their performance. (p. 367)

It is probably unreasonable to expect all teachers, even the majority of teachers, to seek the lofty status of expert. Indeed, the natural human condition appears to be to stop development once an acceptable level of performance has been reached. Ericsson and Charness (1994) explain: "Most amateurs and employees spend a very small amount of time on deliberate practice efforts to improve their performance once it has reached an acceptable level" (p. 730). How, then, could a district or school encourage teachers to continue developing their expertise?

We address this issue in Chapter 7. Briefly, we believe that educators are not motivated by money (although there is certainly nothing wrong with rewarding expertise financially). However, they *are* motivated by recognition of expertise. This idea is not new. National Board certification is designed singularly for this purpose.

Albert Shanker, president of the American Federation of Teachers, is credited with first outlining in 1985 how teaching might be further professionalized through the establishment of an organization that documented and recognized excellence in teaching. The Carnegie Corporation of New York endorsed Shanker's call by establishing the Carnegie Forum on Education and the Economy's Task Force on Teaching as a Profession. In 1987, the Carnegie Corporation funded the establishment of the National Board for Professional Teaching Standards (NBPTS).

Since its inception, NBPTS has grown steadily in popularity. For example, NBPTS certifications granted saw a surge between 2003 and 2007, with 63,800 granted during those years (Viadero & Honawar, 2008). Recent figures indicate that a total of 82,000 teachers have achieved national board certification or recertification (National Board for Professional Teaching Standards, 2010; Estes Park News, 2010). Although there have been some challenges regarding the extent to which NBPTS certification is associated with enhanced student achievement (see Sawchuck, 2009, 2010; Thirunarayanan, 2004; Viadero & Honawar, 2008), its popularity attests to the fact that teachers are motivated by recognition of their expertise. In fact, NBPTS certification actually costs teachers $2,500 to apply and complete the process, yet more and more teachers seek the endorsement every year. In our opinion, such recognition can and should be a regular aspect of the teacher's evaluation process in districts and schools. In Chapter 7, we outline a process whereby teacher evaluation not only recognizes and documents teachers' levels of expertise, but also supports their progress through those levels.

District Support for Developing Expertise

The initiatives described in this book are not easily implemented. They require a redistribution of resources at the district level. They also require a willingness on the part of districts to recognize expertise and a willingness on the part of expert teachers to stand and be counted as leaders. Although our suggestions are ambitious, they are not new. For example, Linda Darling-Hammond (2009) asserts "that all practitioners [should] have the support to become expert" (p. 64). Using different terminology, she calls for a massive refocusing of energy and resources across districts in the United States.

The need for districtwide effort to support teacher expertise has also been highlighted in a study of district leadership. Specifically, in *District Leadership That Works,* which reports on a meta-analysis of research on district leadership, Marzano and Waters (2009) identify five responsibilities of district administrators that had a significant correlation with student achievement. One of these district responsibilities was nonnegotiable goals for instruction. Marzano and Waters assert that one of the more powerful actions district leaders can take to enhance student achievement is to develop a system that encourages, supports, and recognizes teacher expertise.

Summary

This chapter provided the foundation for the recommendations made in this book. It began with the well-established generalization that teacher expertise is causally related to student achievement. The more skilled the teacher, the greater the students' achievement. The nature of expertise was briefly discussed, with an emphasis on the fact that it can be developed with deliberate practice over time. Five conditions for developing teacher expertise were briefly described: (1) a well-articulated knowledge base for teaching, (2) focused feedback and practice,

(3) opportunities to observe and discuss expertise, (4) clear criteria and a plan for success, and (5) providing recognition of expertise. The chapter ended with a discussion of the importance of a districtwide emphasis on improving teacher expertise.

CHAPTER 2

A Brief History of Supervision and Evaluation

Before providing the specific suggestions for the initiatives described in Chapter 1, it is useful to consider the history of teacher supervision and evaluation in the United States. We include the topic of evaluation in our review because it is so commonly linked to supervision.

The Early Days of Supervision and Evaluation

In the 1700s, education was not considered a professional discipline or field of study. Early towns in the United States turned to existing power structures, such as local government and the clergy, to hire teachers and make judgments about their teaching. Clergy were considered logical choices for this role because of their extensive education and presumed ability to guide religious instruction in schools (Tracy, 1995, p. 320). The teacher was considered a servant of the community. Individual supervisors or supervisory committees were charged with monitoring the quality of instruction. These supervisors had nearly unlimited power to establish criteria for effective instruction and to hire and fire teachers (Burke & Krey, 2005). Because there was no necessary agreement as to the importance or nature of pedagogical expertise, the quality and type of feedback to teachers was highly varied.

A rising industrial base and the common schooling movement that extended through the 1800s spawned large urban areas with more complex school systems. In these larger schools and districts, a demand grew for teachers who held expertise in specific disciplines and for administrators who could assume increasingly complex roles. One teacher within a building was often selected to assume administrative duties. This "principal" teacher ultimately grew into the role of building principal.

The trend toward specialized roles started in large urban districts and soon spread to smaller cities and rural areas (Tracy, 1995). About this time, it was acknowledged that clergy didn't necessarily have the knowledge base to make informed judgments about teacher effectiveness. Tracy explains, "Rather than simply understanding the mores of the community, the supervisor now needed to have subject area knowledge and teaching skills" (p. 323). Clearly, clergy were not trained for such a role.

By the mid-1800s, the view of teaching was that it was a complex endeavor requiring complex feedback if expertise was to be fostered. Blumberg (1985) notes that at this time supervision began to focus on improving instruction. He offers the following quote from an 1845 document titled *The Annual Report of the Superintendent of Common Schools of the State of New York*:

> Too much reliance ought not to be placed upon visitation to the schools, to give method to the teacher and efficacy to his instructions. Instruction is the primary object of visitation, and . . . more instruction can be given to teachers of a town when assembled together in one day. (p. 63, as cited in original source of 1845, p. 131)

Blumberg asserts that although supervisors were no longer clergy, they were no less evangelical. Within a given county, superintendents traveled from community to community and school to school, proselytizing for more effective instructional practices. As one superintendent stated, "The only salvation for the republic is to be sought for in our schools" (1845, p. 19, as cited in Blumberg, 1985).

The period from the beginning of formal education in the United States up to the mid-1800s saw the dawning of the awareness that pedagogical skills are a necessary component of effective teaching. Although there was little or no formal discussion about the specifics of these skills, the acknowledgment of their importance might be considered the first step in the journey to a comprehensive approach to developing teacher expertise.

The Period of Scientific Management

The latter part of the 19th century and the early part of the 20th century were dominated by two competing views of education. One was embodied in the writings of John Dewey. Dewey was one of the most prolific writers and thinkers in the field of education in the early 20th century. He saw democracy, not scientific management, as the conceptual underpinning of human progress. He argued that schools should be organized in such a way that students can practice citizenship and further develop the ideals of democracy (Dewey, 1938, 1981). Progressive ideas such as a student-centered education, connecting the classroom to the real world, differentiation based on student learning needs, and integration of content areas were espoused by Dewey as ways of bridging the gap between students' passive role as learners and the active role they would need to play as citizens.

The second view of education was embodied in the work of Frederick Taylor. Taking a scientific view of management, Taylor believed that measurement of specific behaviors of factory workers was perhaps the most powerful means to improve production. He argued that if there were 100 ways to perform a task, some methods would be more efficient than others. By studying the various ways a task such as shoveling coal could be performed, the *one best method* could be determined. According to Taylor (1911), these principles could be applied to discrete tasks such as shoveling coal and to more systemic tasks such as the selection of workers, development of training programs, and processes for dividing labor. Taylor's ideas resonated with engineers and business owners, and colleges of engineering and business were well positioned to infuse his principles into their courses. Taylor's principles also began to have an impact on K–12 education.

Led by Edward Thorndike, educators began to view measurement as the ultimate tool for a more scientific approach to schooling. Thorndike's theories were applied to administration by Ellwood Cubberley. Originally published in 1916, Cubberley's book *Public School Administration* (1929) described how Taylor's principles could be used to manage schools in the same way factories are managed:

> Our schools are, in a sense, factories in which the raw products (children) are to be shaped and fashioned into products to meet the various demands of life. The specifications for manufacturing come from the demands of twentieth century civilization and is the business of the school to build its pupils according to the specifications laid down. (p. 338)

Based on the factory metaphor, Cubberley laid out a set of principles for school administrators that emphasized measurement and analysis of data to ensure that teachers and schools were productive. In the third edition of his book, *Public School Administration* (1929), Cubberley provided specific examples of how a scientific approach could be applied when visiting teachers' classrooms. He described specific feedback that a supervisor might provide to a teacher. For example, on a scale from *A* to *F*, this 6th grade teacher was given a *D* for her arithmetic lesson. Cubberley's supervisory form stated:

> Weak Points: Entirely wrong procedure for type of problems used. No attempt at problem-solving instruction. . . .

> Suggestions Made: Explained to her that, being a new teacher to our schools, she evidently did not know how we taught Arithmetic. Explained faults of the lesson, but commended her managerial ability. Told her how she should handle such work, and gave her Newcomb's Modern Methods of Teaching Arithmetic to take home and read designated chapters. (Cubberley, 1929, p. 327)

Building on Cubberley's work, William Wetzel (1929) proposed using measures of student learning to determine the effectiveness of a teacher or school. These measures were in addition to focusing on a teacher's use of specific strategies and behaviors. However, Wetzel distanced himself from the metaphor of schools as factories with a manufacturing function. He recommended three components as the basis for scientific supervision: the use of aptitude tests to determine the ability level of each child; the establishment of clear, measurable objectives for each course; and the use of reliable measures of student learning.

Through the 1930s, there was continued tension between the scientific approach to schooling, including a greater reliance on standardized tests, and the approach that focused on social development and democratic values. To some extent, this was a false dichotomy. The science of education as proposed by Cubberley and Wetzel dealt more with the feedback system used to determine if teachers, schools, and districts were being effective. To this extent, their emphasis was on data with which to make decisions about future actions. Considered from this perspective, some of Cubberley and Wetzel's recommendations might be considered precursors to some of our recommendations regarding the use of data for feedback. Dewey's focus was more on the ultimate goal of education. The two perspectives are not innately incompatible. One can use data for feedback but still maintain the goal of an education system that fosters democratic ideals. Nonetheless, the two perspectives were not described or perceived in a fashion that allowed for integration, and the tension between them continued through the Great Depression.

Post–World War II

The period immediately after World War II began with a swing away from the scientific approach to schooling. Rather than describing supervisory processes in terms of raw materials and products, the literature began to focus on the teacher *as an individual*. Emphasis was placed on not only assisting the teacher to develop his or her unique skills, but also tending to his or her emotional needs. The January 1946 issue of *Educational Leadership* magazine, published only a few months after the conclusion of World War II, reflects this shift. In an article titled "The Supervisory Visit," Elsie Coleman (1945) stated that "the first fundamental in understanding the teacher is . . . that the teacher is a person, different from every other person, living in an environment which affects and in turn is affected by that person" (p. 165). In the same issue of *Educational Leadership*, Lewis and Leps (1946) described the supervisory process as though it were an extension of efforts to liberate Europe. Guidelines for a successful supervisory model included (1) democratic ideals, (2) opportunities for initiative, (3) understanding human limitations, (4) shared decision making, and (5) delegation of responsibility (p. 163). In describing this new world of supervision, Lewis and Leps stated, "The school administrator, with the acceptance of the community, is gaining the courage to utilize the creative force to be gained in freeing the human beings who comprise the school situation to participate in the making of policies and plans for their execution; and, hence, to utilize the force and creativity inherent in the democratic process" (p. 161).

In spite of the emphasis on the teacher as an individual, the role of the supervisor during this era was defined in rather specific terms. Unfortunately, the list of supervisory responsibilities was quite long and broad. For example, Swearingen (1946) described the role of the supervisor as including the following areas: the curriculum, teaching personnel, the teaching/learning situation, the emotional quality of the classroom, resources and materials of instruction, auxiliary functions including working with the school lunch service, attendance, distribution of textbooks, public relations, and working with cooperative groups and agencies. In his text *Instructional Supervision: A Guide to Modern Practice*, William Melchoir (1950) described supervision as including individual meetings with teachers, faculty meetings, business meetings, social meetings, workshops and other committee meetings in addition to "classroom visitation for observation and study" (p. 51). While classroom visitation is discussed explicitly in Melchoir's text, its relative importance (based on page count in the book) seems to imply that the supervisor's role was more about management of the physical plant than instructional leadership. For example, 23 pages in the book were devoted to "Beautifying Grounds and Buildings" (pp. 107–130), while only 16 pages were devoted to classroom observation (pp. 364–380). Finally, in her article titled "So

Begins—So Ends the Supervisor's Day," Ethel Thompson (1952) added to the growing list of responsibilities by describing the supervisor's role as attending student placement conferences, observing in a classroom, working with parents and principals, completing paperwork, meeting with various school committees, attending student conferences, recruiting new teachers, meeting with various professional organizations, doing demonstration lessons, and acting as a resource to others in the organization.

Although the proliferation of responsibilities for the supervisor was counterproductive at best, one positive outcome from this era was a consensus on the importance and utility of teacher observation. In his article "Teachers Look at Supervision," Matthew Whitehead (1952) described six broad areas of supervision and surveyed teachers as to their perceptions of the importance of each area. Noting the importance of effective classroom observation, he pointed out advances that must be made in observational practices to capitalize on its potential:"Improvements were still needed in following up the visitation with a conference, and in having the principal see the importance of remaining the entire period. It is not fair to teachers to visit them and not hold a conference following the visitation nor is it just to visit in a 'piecemeal' fashion" (p. 102). Whitehead summarized his position by explaining that "administrators should pay more attention to the chief aim of education—effective teaching" (p. 106). It was the recognition of the importance of classroom observation that laid the foundations for one of the most influential movements in supervision.

The Era of Clinical Supervision

Few innovations in the field of education spread as quickly as clinical supervision. Developed in the late 1950s and described in detail in books published in the late 1960s and early 1970s, clinical supervisory models spread like wildfire. By 1980, one study found that about 90 percent of school administrators used some type of clinical supervisory model (Bruce & Hoehn, 1980). Few models in the entire field of education—let alone in the specific domain of educational supervision—have been as widely deployed, as widely disparaged, or as widely misunderstood.

Morris Cogan was a professor and supervisor of candidates in Harvard's Master's of Arts in Teaching (MAT) program in the 1950s. Over years of what might be described, at least in part, as trial and error, he and his colleagues developed a systematic approach to working with student teachers. By 1958, Cogan was lecturing on a process called the "cycle of clinical supervision" (Cogan, 1973). By 1962, a group of educational practitioners working with Cogan in the MAT program had further refined the clinical approach. According to one of those practitioners,

Robert Goldhammer, the model was analogous to supervisory practices used in teaching hospitals. The process involved a purposeful, symbiotic relationship between practitioner and resident, where observation and discussion drove both parties to higher levels of growth and effectiveness (Goldhammer, 1969, p. 54).

The model that emerged from these efforts was published in a book by Goldhammer (1969) entitled *Clinical Supervision: Special Methods for the Supervision of Teachers*. Based on visits to hundreds of classrooms and hundreds of supervisory conferences, Goldhammer developed a five-phase process of clinical supervision that was designed to involve teachers and supervisors in a reflective dialogue.

- *Phase 1—Preobservation Conference:* This phase was designed to provide a conceptual framework for the observation. During this phase, the teacher and supervisor planned the specifics of the observation.
- *Phase 2—Classroom Observation:* During this phase, the supervisor observed the teacher using the framework articulated in Phase 1.
- *Phase 3—Analysis:* Data from the observation was organized by the supervisor with the intent of helping teachers participate "in developing evaluations of their own teaching" (p. 63).
- *Phase 4—A Supervision Conference:* The teacher and supervisor engaged in a dialogue about the data. The teacher was asked to reflect upon and explain his or her professional practice. This stage also could include providing "didactic assistance" (p. 70) to the teacher.
- *Phase 5—Analysis of the Analysis:* The supervisor's "practice was examined with all of the rigor and for basically the same purposes that Teacher's professional behavior was analyzed theretofore" (p. 71).

In 1973, Morris Cogan wrote the book *Clinical Supervision*. As mentioned previously, Cogan was one of Goldhammer's professors at Harvard. His focus was on specific classroom behaviors. He noted that supervisors should be looking for "critical incidents" that "impede desired learnings in striking fashion" (p. 172). He also emphasized the fact that the supervisory process should be viewed as a vital aspect of the process of continual improvement in teaching:

> A cornerstone of the supervisor's work with the teacher is the assumption that clinical supervision constitutes a continuation of the teacher's professional education. This does not mean that the teacher is "in training," as is sometimes said of preservice programs. It means that he is continuously engaged in improving his practice, as is required of all professionals. In this sense, the teacher involved in clinical supervision must be perceived as a practitioner fulfilling one of the first requirements of a professional—maintaining and developing his competence. He must not be treated as a person

being rescued from ineptitude, saved from incompetence, or supported in his stumblings. He must perceive himself to be engaged in the supervisory processes as a professional who continues his education and enlarges his competences. (p. 21)

One of the more interesting aspects of Cogan's perspective was his caution that a supervisor's personal model of teaching might impede his or her ability to provide effective feedback to teachers.

> Most teachers have consciously and unconsciously constructed a personal model of the good teacher. Such conceptions generally grow by accretion rather than by critical examination and careful testing. The result is that too often the operating model of the teacher-turned-supervisor is pretty much what he himself does well. When teachers become supervisors, these personal preferences generally operate in full vigor, furnishing many of the criteria for viewing the teaching of others. (1973, p. 54)

It is instructive to contrast the original view of clinical supervision with that into which it evolved. Goldhammer was clear that what is to be observed is the holistic practice of teaching: the interaction of the teacher and student related to student learning. The five phases of the clinical supervision process were intended to be the vehicle to disclose effective instructional practices. However, over time, the five phases became an end in themselves. In some cases, the rich, trusting dialogue envisioned by Goldhammer was reduced to a ritualistic set of steps to be followed. Perhaps contributing to this problem was Goldhammer's resistance to defining any characteristics of effective instruction. In Goldhammer's view, the supervisor should have few if any preconceived notions of what constitutes effective teaching:

> Since I have deliberately not structured my observations in advance so that, for example, I should only record data in certain predetermined categories, and since I have collected as many data as possible in order to alleviate unconscious selectivity, I must now, ex post facto, invent categories of some kind. I must organize the data into classes of one sort or another in order to talk about them. . . . Categories of behavior have no objective existence of their own; they do not exist independently in the real world; I make them up. (1969, p. 95)

Regardless of the reasons for its demise, Goldhammer's vision of supervision as a collegial, inquiry-driven quest for more effective instructional practices quickly disappeared. The five phases of the clinical model, absent the rich dialogue proposed by Goldhammer, became the de facto structure for the evaluation of teachers—clearly a purpose for which it was not intended.

The Hunter Model

The next major influence on supervision was the work of Madeline Hunter (1980, 1984). The centerpiece of her work was the seven-step model of a lesson depicted in Figure 2.1.

Although the seven-step framework for a lesson is the most well-known aspect of Hunter's work, she contributed many other ideas to the process of supervision. For example, she championed the idea of using professional development to articulate a common language of instruction. She also identified a variety of purposes for supervisory conferences that included the following:

- To identify, label, and explain instructional behaviors as related to research;
- To encourage teachers to consider alternative approaches that are aligned to their style of teaching;
- To help teachers identify components of lessons that were not as effective as they had hoped;
- To identify and describe "less effective aspects of teaching that were not evident to the teacher" (1980, p. 410);
- To promote the continued growth of excellent teachers;
- To evaluate "what has occurred in and resulted from a series of instructional conferences" supportable by objective evidence rather than based on subjective opinion (1980, p. 412).

Observation and script taping were critical components of Hunter's process of supervision. During script taping, a supervisor recorded teaching behaviors and then later categorized them into those that "promoted learning; those that used precious time and energy, yet contributed nothing to learning; and those that, unintentionally, actually interfered with learning" (Hunter, 1980, p. 409). After script taping, supervisors conferred with teachers. During this postconference, the supervisor and teacher discussed the data from the script taping in depth.

In short order, Hunter's seven elements of an effective lesson became the prescription for teacher evaluation in many states (Fehr, 2001, p. 175). If clinical supervision was the prescribed structure of supervision, Hunter's seven-step model, referred to as *mastery teaching,* became the content of the preconference, observation, and postconference. Teachers described their lessons in terms of Hunter's model, and supervisors determined the effectiveness of observed lessons in terms of alignment to the model.

FIGURE 2.1	The Hunter Model of Lesson Design

Element	Description
Anticipatory set	A mental set that causes students to focus on what will be learned. It may also give practice in helping students achieve the learning and yield diagnostic data for the teacher. *Example:* "Look at the paragraph on the board. What do you think might be the most important part to remember?"
Objective and purpose	Not only do students *learn* more effectively when they know what they're supposed to be learning and why that learning is important to them, but teachers *teach* more effectively when they have that same information. *Example:* "Frequently people have difficulty in remembering things that are important to them. Sometimes you feel you have studied hard and yet don't remember some of the important parts. Today, we're going to learn ways to identify what's important, and then we'll practice ways we can use to remember important things."
Input	Students must acquire new information about the knowledge, process, or skill they are to achieve. To design the input phase of the lesson so that a successful outcome becomes predictable, the teacher must have analyzed the final objective to identify knowledge and skills that need to be acquired.
Modeling	"Seeing" what is meant is an important adjunct to learning. To avoid stifling creativity, showing several examples of the process or products that students are expected to acquire or produce is helpful.
Checking for understanding	Before students are expected to do something, the teacher should determine that they understand what they are supposed to do and that they have the minimum skills required.
Guided practice	Students practice their new knowledge or skill *under direct teacher supervision.* New learning is like wet cement; it is easily damaged. An error at the beginning of learning can easily "set" so that correcting it later is harder than correcting it immediately.
Independent practice	Independent practice is assigned only after the teacher is reasonably sure that students will not make serious errors. After an initial lesson, students are frequently not ready to practice independently, and the teacher has committed a pedagogical error if unsupervised practice is expected.

Source: Adapted from M. Hunter (1984), "Knowing, Teaching, and Supervising." In P. Hosford (Ed.), *Using What We Know About Teaching* (pp. 169–192). Alexandria, VA: ASCD.

The Era of Developmental/Reflective Models

By the mid-1980s, researchers and theorists in supervision began to articulate alternative perspectives, primarily in reaction to the prescription applications of clinical supervision and mastery teaching. William Glatthorn promoted supervisory models that considered a teacher's career goals. In *Differentiated Supervision,* Glatthorn (1984) explained that as professionals, teachers should have input and some sense of control over their development. Through differentiation, supervisors were expected to focus clinical supervisory practices on staff members who would derive the greatest benefit from a clinical approach. Additionally, different opportunities and venues for professional growth were to be provided for teachers based on their individual needs.

In a similar vein, Thomas McGreal (1983) delineated a range of supervisory options based on teacher experience. These options ranged from intensive developmental supervision for nontenured teachers and teachers with significant instructional deficiencies to more self-directed professional development for experienced staff. For evaluation purposes, McGreal recommended that teachers be placed either in an intensive evaluation program designed to make high-stakes decisions related to continued employment or granting of tenure, or in a standard evaluation program designed for quality assurance.

Another proponent of the differentiated approach to supervision during this era was Carl Glickman. In the first edition of his book *Supervision of Instruction: A Developmental Approach,* Glickman (1985) affirmed that the most important goal of supervision was to improve instruction. In the fouth edition of his book (1998), he described a number of related actions that constitute a robust approach to supervision. They included "(1) direct assistance to teachers, (2) group development, (3) professional development, (4) curriculum development, and (5) action research" (p. xv). Glickman noted that to implement a robust model of supervision, educators must take a systemic approach to the supervisory process: "By understanding how teachers grow optimally in a supportive and challenging environment, the supervisor can plan the tasks of supervision to bring together organizational goals and teacher needs into a single fluid entity" (1998, p. 10).

Clearly this era saw substantive arguments against the rigid applications of clinical supervision and mastery teaching. This era also set the stage for an emphasis on teacher evaluation.

The RAND Study

Amid the debates about the proper approach to supervision in the 1980s, the RAND group engaged in a study to determine what types of supervisory and evaluation practices were actually occurring in school districts across the United States. Its report, titled *Teacher Evaluation: A Study of Effective Practices* (Wise, Darling-Hammond, McLaughlin, & Bernstein, 1984), found that many of the systems of supervision and evaluation in place at this time were quite didactic and formulaic in nature. One general finding from the study was that the supervisory and evaluative approaches that were more developmental and reflective were sometimes viewed as not specific enough to enhance pedagogical development. Indeed, the report stated that teachers were the strongest advocates for more standardized processes. "In their view, narrative evaluation provided insufficient information about the standards and criteria against which teachers were evaluated and resulted in inconsistent ratings among schools" (Wise et al., 1984, p. 16). The models in place in most of the 32 districts they studied were adopted or developed through committees of teachers, administrators, union representatives, and principals.

Four consistent problems with supervision and evaluation were also identified in the study. Nearly all respondents felt that principals "lacked sufficient resolve and competence to evaluate accurately" (Wise et al., 1984, p. 22). Teacher resistance to feedback was the second most identified problem. A key source of this resistance was related to the third most identified problem: a lack of uniform evaluation practices. The hypothesized reason for this concern was the fact that of the 32 districts in the study, only one district had a system built on a set of established teacher competencies. The fourth problem was a lack of training for evaluators. The study authors summarized their findings in four conclusions and 12 recommendations. These are reported in Figure 2.2.

The Danielson Model

In 1996, a seminal work on supervision and evaluation was published by Charlotte Danielson. *Enhancing Professional Practice: A Framework for Teaching*, which was updated in 2007, was based on her work with the Educational Testing Service that focused on measuring the competence of preservice teachers. Given its past and current popularity, the Danielson model must be the reference point for any new proposals regarding supervision and evaluation. Whereas Hunter had described steps in the teaching process and Goldhammer and Cogan had done the same for the supervisory process, Danielson sought to capture—in its full complexity—the dynamic process of classroom teaching.

As we briefly described in Chapter 1, Danielson's model included four domains: Planning and Preparation, the Classroom Environment, Instruction, and Professional Responsibilities. Within each of these domains, she described a series of components that further articulate the knowledge, skills, and dispositions required to demonstrate competence in the classroom. According to Danielson (1996), the intent of the framework was to accomplish three things. First, it sought to honor the complexity of teaching. Second, it constituted a language

| FIGURE 2.2 | Conclusions and Recommendations from the RAND Study |

Conclusion	Recommendation
"To succeed, a teacher evaluation system must suit the educational goals, management style, conception of teaching, and community values of the school district" (Wise et al., 1984, p. 66).	• Examine goals and purpose of educational system and align system to those ends. • States should not adopt highly prescriptive systems (Wise et al., 1984).
"Top-level commitment to and resource for evaluation outweigh checklists and procedures" (Wise et al., 1984, p. 67).	• Provide administrators with adequate time for evaluations. • The quality of evaluation and ability of evaluators should be monitored. • Training for evaluators is important, particularly with new systems (Wise et al., 1984).
"The school district must decide the main purpose of its teacher evaluation system and then match the process to the purpose" (Wise et al., 1984, p. 70).	• Examine current systems to determine and align with primary purpose. • Consider adopting multiple systems if there are different purposes (Wise et al., 1984).
"To sustain resource commitments and political support, teacher evaluation must be seen to have utility. Utility depends on the efficient use of resources to achieve reliability, validity, and cost effectiveness" (Wise et al., 1984, p. 73).	• Allocate resources as aligned to importance of purpose. • Target resources to achieve maximum results (Wise et al., 1984).
"Teacher involvement and responsibility improve the quality of teacher evaluation" (Wise et al., 1984, p. 76).	• Involve expert teachers in the supervision and assistance of peers. • Involve teacher organizations in the development of processes and ongoing monitoring. • Hold teachers accountable for instructional decisions (Wise et al., 1984).

for professional conversation. Third, it provided a structure for self-assessment and reflection on professional practice. The framework was considered comprehensive by Danielson in that it included all phases of teaching—from planning to reporting achievement. Additionally, Danielson noted that the model was grounded in research and that it is generic or flexible enough to be used across levels and disciplines.

One of the more powerful aspects of the Danielson framework was that each of the 76 elements of quality teaching was broken into four levels of performance (unsatisfactory, basic, proficient, and distinguished). An example of one of these elements and the corresponding levels of performance is reported in Figure 2.3.

The level of specificity supplied in the Danielson model provided the foundation for the most detailed and comprehensive approach to evaluation to that time.

FIGURE 2.3	Component from Danielson's Model

DOMAIN 2: THE CLASSROOM ENVIRONMENT

Component 2b: Establishing a Culture for Learning

Element	Unsatisfactory	Basic	Proficient	Distinguished
Expectations for learning and achievement	Instructional outcomes, activities and assignments, and classroom interactions convey low expectations for at least some students.	Instructional outcomes, activities and assignments, and classroom interactions convey only modest expectations for student learning and achievement.	Instructional outcomes, activities and assignments, and classroom interactions convey high expectations for most students.	Instructional outcomes, activities and assignments, and classroom interactions convey high expectations for all students. Students appear to have internalized these expectations.

Source: From *Enhancing Professional Practice: A Framework for Teaching* (p. 69) by C. Danielson, 2007, Alexandria, VA: ASCD. Copyright 2007 by ASCD.

The Beginning of the 21st Century

Since the turn of the 21st century, emphasis has shifted from supervision to evaluation, as well as from teacher behavior to student achievement. In their 2005 book *Linking Teacher Evaluation and Student Learning*, Tucker and Stronge championed the importance of student achievement as a criterion in the evaluation process. Specifically, they argued for evaluation systems that determine teacher effectiveness using evidence from student gains in learning as well as observations of classroom instruction. To study how both of these components can be valued concurrently, they examined the supervisory systems in four different school districts that used data on instructional practices and learning gains. They drew a series of recommendations supporting the use of both types of data. However, their recommendations regarding the use of student achievement data were the most forcefully stated: "Given the clear and undeniable link that exists between teacher effectiveness and student learning, we support the use of student achievement information in teacher assessment. Student achievement can, and indeed should be, an important source of feedback on the effectiveness of schools, administrators, and teachers" (p. 102).

In 2008, Toch and Rothman's report *Rush to Judgment* provided a provocative perspective on teacher evaluation. They critiqued current supervisory and evaluative practices, saying they are "superficial, capricious, and often don't even directly address the quality of instruction, much less measure students' learning" (p. 1). Specifically, they described teaching as a profession that focuses on formal credentials rather than on instructional effectiveness and student achievement. Furthermore, despite No Child Left Behind requirements around teacher quality, they found only 14 states that required school systems to do annual evaluations of teachers. They noted that some evaluation systems may not even reflect teacher effectiveness in the classroom. Michigan State professor Mary Kennedy is quoted as saying, "in most instances, it's nothing more than marking satisfactory or unsatisfactory" (p. 2).

In 2009, a similar study entitled *The Widget Effect* (Weisberg, Sexton, Mulhern, & Keeling, 2009) heavily criticized teacher evaluation practices in the United States. The report authors explained its unusual name in the following way:

> The failure of evaluation systems to provide accurate and credible information about individual teachers' instructional performance sustains and reinforces a phenomenon that we have come to call the **Widget Effect**. The Widget Effect describes the tendency of school districts to assume classroom effectiveness is the same from teacher to teacher. This decades-old fallacy fosters an environment in which teachers cease to be understood as individual professionals, but rather as interchangeable parts. In its denial of individual strengths and weaknesses, it is deeply disrespectful to teachers; in its indifference to instructional effectiveness, it gambles with the lives of students. (p. 4)

The *Widget Effect* was the product of research into the evaluation practices in 12 districts across four states including approximately 15,000 teachers, 1,300 administrators, and more than 80 local and state education officials. Specific findings indicated major flaws in the teacher evaluation process:

> The failure to assess variations in instructional effectiveness also precludes districts from identifying specific development needs in their teachers. In fact, 73 percent of teachers surveyed said their most recent evaluation did not identify any development areas, and only 45 percent of teachers who did have development areas identified said they received useful support to improve. (p. 6)

Final conclusions from the report suggested a complete overhaul of the teacher evaluation process:

Evaluations are short and infrequent (most are based on two or fewer class-room observations totaling 60 minutes or less), conducted by untrained administrators, and influenced by powerful cultural forces—in particular, an expectation among teachers that they will be among the vast majority rated as top performers.

While it is impossible to know whether the system drives the culture or the culture the system, the result is clear—evaluation systems fail to differenti-ate performance among teachers. As a result, teacher effectiveness is largely ignored. Excellent teachers cannot be recognized or rewarded, chronically low-performing teachers languish, and the wide majority of teachers perform-ing at moderate levels do not get the differentiated support and development they need to improve as professionals. (p. 6)

Clearly, by the end of the first decade of the 21st century, teacher evaluation practices were under siege.

Lessons from History

The history of supervision and evaluation in this country can be viewed as a gradual evolution to the recommendations we make in this book. A well-articu-lated knowledge base for teaching is supported by the successes of the Hunter model and the utility of the Danielson model. Their specificity was their strength. However, as evidenced by the misuses of clinical supervision, history has taught us that a well-articulated knowledge base should not be used as a prescription for teaching or teacher evaluation. Focused feedback and practice are supported by the development of reflective supervisory models proposed by Glatthorn, McGreal, and Glickman. True pedagogical development comes from teacher self-reflection that results in clear goals for improvement. Clear criteria for success that involve both teacher behavior and student achievement have roots in the emphases in the first decade of the 21st century on student achievement as the ultimate criterion for teacher effectiveness with teacher behavior as a causal fac-tor. Finally, recognizing expertise is also supported by the emphasis on teacher evaluation in the first decade of the 21st century. If student achievement is not linked to teacher evaluation, teachers have little incentive to develop into experts.

The only aspect of our model that is not supported by the history of supervi-sion and evaluation is providing opportunities to observe and discuss expertise. Probably the closest support for this aspect of our model is found in Glickman's perspective that supervision should be a systemic process. Teaching occurs within the context of a community; supervision and evaluation should be supported by that community.

Summary

This chapter presented a brief discussion of the history of teacher supervision and evaluation in the United States. The early days of supervision and evaluation began in the 1700s and lasted until the mid-1800s. They were characterized by a reliance on clergy to provide guidance to and supervision of teachers. As school systems became more complex, the need for more specialized guidance for teachers gave rise to the principal teacher as leader and a growing awareness of the importance of pedagogy. The era of scientific management, from the late 1800s until right before World War II, was characterized by two competing views of education. One was the view that the purpose of education was the promotion of democratic ideals. The other was the view that schools function best when approached from the perspective of scientific management. Throughout this era, the scientific approach gained strength and acceptance. The period after World War II saw a swing away from the scientific approach to an emphasis on developing the teacher as an individual. This period also saw a proliferation of the responsibilities of the supervisor.

The next era, lasting from the late 1960s to the early 1970s, saw the phenomenon of clinical supervision—one of the most influential movements in supervision and evaluation. The Hunter model was combined with clinical supervision to produce a widely used but oftentimes prescriptive approach to supervision. This period was followed by developmental/reflective models that were much less prescriptive. The RAND study provided a realistic look at the actual practice of supervision and evaluation in districts and schools and concluded that teachers preferred specific as opposed to general feedback.

The mid-1990s saw the introduction of the Danielson model to teacher supervision and evaluation. It was widely applied through K–12 education. Finally, the first decade of the 21st century witnessed heavy criticisms of current evaluation practices calling for major changes in tenure and compensation.

CHAPTER 3

A Knowledge Base for Teaching

As described in Chapter 1, a knowledge base for teaching is the first step a district or school must take if it is to support the development of teacher expertise. The model we propose has four domains: (1) classroom strategies and behaviors, (2) planning and preparing, (3) reflecting on teaching, and (4) collegiality and professionalism. Each domain has subcategories; and in the case of the first domain, classroom strategies and behaviors, the subcategories themselves have subcategories. The complete model is depicted in Figure 3.1.

Across the four domains are 60 specific elements, when one considers the most specific level of organization (i.e., 41 elements in Domain 1, 8 elements in Domain 2, 5 elements in Domain 3, and 6 elements in Domain 4). In terms of sheer quantity of elements, this is similar to the Danielson model, which has 76 elements. However, our emphasis is different.

Specifically, Domain 1 of Figure 3.1 involves over half of the elements in the model—41 of the total 60. This imbalance reflects the importance we place on classroom strategies and behaviors. As depicted in Figure 1.2 in Chapter 1, Domain 1 has a direct causal link with student achievement. Additionally, this domain is the most complex. It has three superordinate categories with nine subcategories embedded within the three superordinate categories.

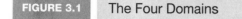

| FIGURE 3.1 | The Four Domains |

DOMAIN 1: CLASSROOM STRATEGIES AND BEHAVIORS

Routine Segments

Design Question 1: What will I do to establish and communicate learning goals, track student progress, and celebrate success?

1. Providing clear learning goals and scales to measure those goals
2. Tracking student progress
3. Celebrating student success

Design Question 6: What will I do to establish and maintain classroom routines?

4. Establishing classroom routines
5. Organizing the physical layout of the classroom for learning

Content Segments

Design Question 2: What will I do to help students effectively interact with new knowledge?
1. Identifying critical information
2. Organizing students to interact with new knowledge
3. Previewing new content
4. Chunking content into "digestible bites"
5. Group processing of new information
6. Elaborating on new information
7. Recording and representing knowledge
8. Reflecting on learning

Design Question 3: What will I do to help students practice and deepen their understanding of new knowledge?

9. Reviewing content
10. Organizing students to practice and deepen knowledge
11. Using homework
12. Examining similarities and differences
13. Examining errors in reasoning
14. Practicing skills, strategies, and processes
15. Revising knowledge

Design Question 4: What will I do to help students generate and test hypotheses about new knowledge?

16. Organizing students for cognitively complex tasks
17. Engaging students in cognitively complex tasks involving hypothesis generating and testing
18. Providing resources and guidance

Segments Enacted on the Spot

Design Question 5: What will I do to engage students?

1. Noticing and reacting when students are not engaged
2. Using academic games
3. Managing response rates during questioning
4. Using physical movement
5. Maintaining a lively pace
6. Demonstrating intensity and enthusiasm
7. Using friendly controversy
8. Providing opportunities for students to talk about themselves
9. Presenting unusual or intriguing information

Design Question 7: What will I do to recognize and acknowledge adherence or lack of adherence to classroom rules and procedures?

10. Demonstrating "withitness"
11. Applying consequences
12. Acknowledging adherence to rules and procedures

Design Question 8: What will I do to establish and maintain effective relationships with students?

13. Understanding students' interests and background
14. Using behaviors that indicate affection for students
15. Displaying objectivity and control

Design Question 9: What will I do to communicate high expectations for all students?

16. Demonstrating value and respect for low-expectancy students
17. Asking questions of low-expectancy students
18. Probing incorrect answers with low-expectancy students

————————————— **DOMAIN 2: PLANNING AND PREPARING** —————————————

Planning and Preparing for Lessons and Units

1. Planning and preparing for effective scaffolding of information within lessons
2. Planning and preparing for lessons within a unit that progress toward a deep understanding and transfer of content
3. Planning and preparing for appropriate attention to established content standards

Planning and Preparing for Use of Materials and Technology

1. Planning and preparing for the use of available materials for upcoming units and lessons (e.g., manipulatives, videotapes)
2. Planning and preparing for the use of available technologies such as interactive whiteboards, response systems, and computers

---

FIGURE 3.1 | The Four Domains (*continued*)

Planning and Preparing for Special Needs of Students

1. Planning and preparing for the needs of English language learners
2. Planning and preparing for the needs of special education students
3. Planning and preparing for the needs of students who come from home environments that offer little support for schooling

---

DOMAIN 3: REFLECTING ON TEACHING

Evaluating Personal Performance

1. Identifying specific areas of pedagogical strength and weakness within Domain 1
2. Evaluating the effectiveness of individual lessons and units
3. Evaluating the effectiveness of specific pedagogical strategies and behaviors across different categories of students (i.e., different socioeconomic groups, different ethnic groups)

Developing and Implementing a Professional Growth Plan

1. Developing a written growth and development plan
2. Monitoring progress relative to the professional growth plan

---

DOMAIN 4: COLLEGIALITY AND PROFESSIONALISM

Promoting a Positive Environment

1. Promoting positive interactions about colleagues
2. Promoting positive interactions about students and parents

Promoting Exchange of Ideas and Strategies

1. Seeking mentorship for areas of need or interest
2. Mentoring other teachers and sharing ideas and strategies

Promoting District and School Development

1. Adhering to district and school rules and procedures
2. Participating in district and school initiatives

This is not to say that the other domains are unimportant. Indeed, as depicted in Figure 1.2 in Chapter 1, Domain 2—planning and preparing—is hypothesized to have a direct link to teacher behavioral changes in the classroom (Domain 1), and reflecting on teaching (Domain 3) is hypothesized to have a direct link to planning and preparing (Domain 2). Of the four domains, the one that has the least direct link with classroom strategies and behaviors is collegiality and professionalism, although the case can be made that Domain 4 is the foundation on which the other domains build. In this chapter, we describe the specific elements in each domain.

Domain 1: Classroom Strategies and Behaviors

This domain directly addresses what teachers do in classrooms. The categories of strategies and behaviors in this domain are taken from *The Art and Science of Teaching* (Marzano, 2007). It was designed as a comprehensive framework that includes the research-based strategies from three related works: *Classroom Instruction That Works* (Marzano, Pickering, & Pollock, 2001), *Classroom Management That Works* (Marzano, Pickering, & Marzano, 2003), and *Classroom Assessment and Grading That Work* (Marzano, 2006). At one level, *The Art and Science of Teaching* is intended as a general framework that teachers can use to remind themselves of research-based strategies. For this purpose, it is best to think of *The Art and Science of Teaching* as a planning framework. This use is shown in Figure 3.2.

| **FIGURE 3.2** | Design Questions from *The Art and Science of Teaching* |

1. What will I do to establish and communicate learning goals, track student progress, and celebrate success?
2. What will I do to help students effectively interact with new knowledge?
3. What will I do to help students practice and deepen their understanding of new knowledge?
4. What will I do to help students generate and test hypotheses about new knowledge?
5. What will I do to engage students?
6. What will I do to establish or maintain classroom rules and procedures?
7. What will I do to recognize and acknowledge adherence and lack of adherence to classroom rules and procedures?
8. What will I do to establish and maintain effective relationships with students?
9. What will I do to communicate high expectations for all students?
10. What will I do to develop effective lessons organized into a cohesive unit?

© 2011 Robert J. Marzano

When planning for instruction, the 10 design questions in Figure 3.2 can be considered somewhat in isolation. They are simply reminders to teachers of classroom strategies and behaviors they might employ in an upcoming lesson or unit. For example, after perusing the 10 design questions in Figure 3.2 while preparing for an upcoming lesson, a teacher might decide that she will focus on Design Questions 2, 5, and 8. That is, the teacher realizes that the ensuing lesson will include new knowledge—content that students have not been exposed to previously. Consequently, she will use some of the strategies from *The Art and Science of Teaching* that are most useful when new content is being introduced (Design Question 2). Additionally, the teacher decides that she will use some engagement strategies (Design Question 5) because she has recently noticed that her students seem to be bored frequently. Finally, the teacher decides to use some strategies to enhance her relationship with students (Design Question 8), particularly those who appear to be alienated from the rest of the group.

While the 10 design questions can be approached independently when planning instruction, they must be reorganized to reflect the natural flow of activity in the classroom when used as a vehicle to enhance teacher expertise through feedback. To this end, the design questions can be organized under three general types of lesson segments: routine segments, content segments, and segments that are enacted on the spot. These segments are the major categories for Domain 1 in Figure 3.1.

A lesson segment is an event in the classroom that has a specific purpose and a specific set of teacher behaviors and strategies that are designed to meet that purpose. We use the term *lesson segment* because it defines a unit of analysis that is particularly useful when providing feedback to teachers. In fact, the term has been used for quite some time. Drawing on a considerable amount of design theory (see Berliner, 1986; Doyle, 1986; Good, Grouws, & Ebmeier, 1983; Leinhardt & Greeno, 1986; Stodolsky, 1983), Leinhardt (1990) proposed the lesson segment as a way of classifying the myriad strategies and behaviors employed by expert teachers:

> This research-based information points to the fact that lessons are constructed with multiple parts, or lesson segments, each of which has important characteristics. Each segment contains different roles for teachers and students. Each segment has multiple goals, which can be more or less successfully met by a variety of actions. Further, these segments are supported by fluid, well-rehearsed routines. (pp. 21–22)

As shown in Figure 3.1, Design Questions 1 and 6 are classified as routine segments that occur daily in every class or at least periodically in classes. Design Questions 2, 3, and 4 deal with content segments. They represent different ways of approaching academic content. Design Questions 5, 7, 8, and 9 address behaviors that must be enacted on the spot. Note that design Question 10 is not listed in Figure 3.1. This is because it deals with unit design and lesson design, which are integral parts of Domain 2—planning and preparing. We begin the discussion of Domain 1 with routine segments.

Routine Segments

Every day in every classroom, teachers expect students to follow certain routines regardless of the content being taught or the age of the students. The Art and Science of Teaching framework includes two categories of routines: (1) communicating learning goals, tracking student progress, and celebrating success; and (2) establishing or maintaining classroom rules and procedures. These categories represent Design Questions 1 and 6, respectively.

Communicating Learning Goals, Tracking Student Progress, and Celebrating Success

Each of the design questions in *The Art and Science of Teaching* (Marzano, 2007) are themselves an amalgamation of a number of instructional strategies and behaviors. The strategies for communicating learning goals, tracking student progress, and celebrating success are supported by research on the effects of goal setting (Lipsey & Wilson, 1993; Walberg, 1999; Wise & Okey, 1983), feedback (Bangert-Drowns, Kulik, Kulik, & Morgan, 1991; Haas, 2005; Hattie & Timperley, 2007; Kumar, 1991), reinforcing effort (Hattie, Biggs, & Purdie 1996; Kumar, 1991; Schunk & Cox, 1986), use of praise (Bloom, 1976; Wilkinson, 1981), and use of rewards (Deci, Ryan, & Koestner, 2001). Specific strategies and behaviors associated with this type of segment include the following:

• Providing clear learning goals and scales to measure those goals (e.g., the teacher provides or reminds students about a specific learning goal)

• Tracking student progress (e.g., using formative assessment, the teacher helps students chart their individual and group progress on a learning goal)

• Celebrating student success (e.g., the teacher helps students acknowledge and celebrate their current status on a learning goal as well as knowledge gain)

To illustrate how these strategies and behaviors might manifest in the classroom, consider a physical education teacher who daily reminds students of the learning goals for the unit. Routinely, if not daily, the teacher helps students track their progress regarding the learning goals for the unit using various types of formative assessment. Throughout the unit and at the end of the unit, the teacher provides opportunities for students to celebrate their knowledge gain as well as their current achievement status.

Establishing or Maintaining Classroom Rules and Procedures

Establishing or maintaining classroom rules and procedures is another type of routine behavior. The strategies and behaviors from this segment are based on the well-researched generalization that procedures should be established early on in the school year and then reviewed and reconsidered in a logical and systematic fashion throughout the school year (Anderson, Evertson, & Emmer, 1980; Brophy & Evertson, 1976; Eisenhart, 1977; Emmer, Evertson, & Anderson, 1980; Good & Brophy, 2003; Moskowitz & Hayman, 1976). Specific strategies and behaviors associated with this type of segment include the following:

- Establishing classroom routines (e.g., the teacher reminds students of a rule or procedure or establishes a new rule or procedure)
- Organizing the physical layout of the classroom for learning (e.g., the teacher organizes materials, traffic patterns, and displays to enhance learning)

To illustrate how these strategies and behaviors might manifest in the classroom, consider an elementary language arts teacher who takes time at the beginning of the school year to establish clear rules and procedures regarding appropriate behavior in the classroom. Additionally, as a matter of routine, the teacher systematically reviews these rules and procedures, making changes as necessary. Finally, the teacher helps establish order by organizing classroom materials, displays, and traffic patterns in a manner that supports learning.

Content Segments

There are three types of content segments: (1) segments that introduce new content, (2) segments that help students practice and deepen their knowledge, and (3) segments that help students apply their knowledge by generating and testing hypotheses. These segments represent Design Questions 2, 3, and 4, respectively. Each of these three segments might manifest as a distinct lesson, although more than one type of content segment may be addressed in a single class period—especially when classes are extended due to block scheduling.

Introducing New Content

Some content lesson segments focus on introducing new content. The strategies and behaviors important to these segments draw from the research on presentation formats (Nuthall, 1999), previewing new content (Ausubel, 1968; Mayer, 1989, 2003; West & Fensham, 1976), organizing new knowledge for efficient processing (Linden et al., 2003; Rosenshine, 2002), summarizing new information (Anderson & Hidi, 1988/1989; Hidi & Anderson, 1987), representing new knowledge in multiple ways (Alvermann & Boothby, 1986; Aubusson, Foswill, Barr, &

Perkovic, 1997; Druyan, 1997; Newton, 1995; Sadoski & Paivio, 2001; Welch, 1997), questioning techniques (Pressley et al., 1992; Reder, 1980; Redfield & Rousseau, 1981), and student self-reflection (Cross, 1998). Specific strategies and behaviors associated with introducing new content include the following:

- Identifying critical information (e.g., the teacher provides cues as to which information is important)
- Organizing students to interact with new knowledge (e.g., the teacher organizes students into dyads or triads to discuss small chunks of content)
- Previewing new content (e.g., the teacher uses strategies such as K-W-L, advance organizers, and preview questions)
- Chunking content into "digestible bites" (e.g., the teacher presents content in small portions that are tailored to students' level of understanding)
- Group processing of new information (e.g., after each chunk of information, the teacher asks students to summarize and clarify what they have experienced)
- Elaborating on new information (e.g., the teacher asks questions that require students to make and defend inferences)
- Recording and representing knowledge (e.g., the teacher asks students to summarize, take notes, or use nonlinguistic representations)
- Reflecting on learning (e.g., the teacher asks students to reflect on what they understand or what they are still confused about)

To illustrate how these strategies and behaviors might manifest in the classroom, consider a social studies teacher who is introducing new information about the concept of dictatorship. The teacher previews the concept by asking students what they remember or think they know about dictatorships. As students volunteer answers, she records their responses on the whiteboard. Using an interactive whiteboard, she shows a DVD clip that illustrates defining characteristics of a dictatorship. Prior to showing the clip, the teacher has organized students into groups of three. She plays about two minutes of the clip and then stops and asks one student in each group of three to summarize what they have seen so far. The other two students in each group ask questions that are posed to the teacher if they are not satisfactorily answered in the triad. Next, the teacher plays another minute of the video and repeats the same process, beginning by having one student in each triad summarize the content. In all, she stops the video four times. Next the teacher asks some questions of the entire class that require students to make inferences about dictatorships. Each triad then develops a summary of the content in the video along with a graphic or pictographic representation of their summaries. At the end of the lesson, students are asked to respond to the following question in their academic notebooks: "What am I still confused about?" This task helps them reflect on what they have learned.

Practicing and Deepening Knowledge

Once new content has been introduced, it must be practiced and deepened if students are to use it independently. The strategies and behaviors important to this type of content lesson segment draw from the research on practice (Kumar, 1991; Ross, 1988), revising and analyzing errors (Halpern, 1984; Hillocks, 1986; Rovee-Collier, 1995), examining similarities and differences (Halpern, Hansen, & Reifer, 1990; McDaniel & Donnelly, 1996), and homework (Cooper, Robinson, & Patall, 2006). Specific strategies and behaviors associated with segments devoted to practicing and deepening knowledge include the following:

- Reviewing content (e.g., the teacher briefly reviews related content addressed previously)
- Organizing students to practice and deepen knowledge (e.g., the teacher organizes students into groups designed to review information or practice skills)
- Using homework (e.g., the teacher uses homework for independent practice or to elaborate on information)
- Examining similarities and differences (e.g., the teacher engages students in comparing, classifying, and creating analogies and metaphors)
- Examining errors in reasoning (e.g., the teacher asks students to examine informal fallacies, propaganda, and bias)
- Practicing skills, strategies, and processes (the teacher uses massed and distributed practice)
- Revising knowledge (e.g., the teacher asks students to revise entries in notebooks to clarify and add to previous information)

To illustrate how these behaviors might manifest, it is useful to distinguish between two types of knowledge: procedural knowledge and declarative knowledge. Procedural knowledge includes skills, strategies, and processes. Declarative knowledge includes details, sequences of information, generalizations, and principles (Marzano & Kendall, 2007). To address procedural knowledge, consider a primary language arts teacher who has previously presented a strategy for editing a composition to make sure there is a clear beginning, middle, and end. To address declarative knowledge, consider a middle school history teacher who has previously presented students with information about republics as a form of government. Both might begin their knowledge practice and deepening segment with a brief review of what was initially presented about the content in the introductory lesson. Both might also organize students into small groups to facilitate the processing of information. The language arts teacher would engage students in some type of practice activity, whereas the history teacher would engage students in some other type of activity designed to provide a deeper understanding of the content. This difference is because procedural knowledge is *practiced,* whereas declarative knowledge is *deepened.* For example, as a practice activity, the language arts teacher might provide students with a set of sample compositions, none of which have clear beginnings, middles, or ends. Individually or in small groups, students would use these contrived examples to practice the revising strategy by rewriting the compositions to include an effective beginning, middle, and end. The history teacher, on the other hand, might have students engage in a comparison activity designed to help students contrast republics with other forms of government. For example, the teacher might ask students to contrast republics with democracies and monarchies. Finally, both teachers might extend the activities begun in class as homework.

Generating and Testing Hypotheses (Applying Knowledge)

The final type of content lesson segment involves activities that require students to apply what they have learned by generating and testing hypotheses. Strategies and behaviors for this type of segment are drawn from the research on problem-based learning (Gijbels, Dochy, Van den Bossche, & Segers, 2005) and hypothesis generation and testing (Hattie et al., 1996; Ross, 1988). Specific strategies and behaviors associated with lesson segments devoted to applying knowledge include the following:

- Organizing students for cognitively complex tasks (e.g., the teacher organizes students into small groups to facilitate cognitively complex tasks)
- Engaging students in cognitively complex tasks involving hypothesis generating and testing (e.g., the teacher engages students in decision-making tasks, problem-solving tasks, experimental inquiry tasks, and investigation tasks)
- Providing resources and guidance (e.g., the teacher makes resources available that are specific to cognitively complex tasks and helps students execute such tasks)

To illustrate how these strategies and behaviors might manifest in the classroom, consider a mathematics teacher who has previously introduced an algorithm for performing three-column addition. As a way of extending students' knowledge, the teacher asks them to experiment with different ways to add three-digit numbers. For example, the teacher might pose the question "What would happen if you started with the last column to the left as opposed to the first column to the right?" Students would first predict how the proposed process of adding three-digit numbers might be affected by the change and then try out this alternative strategy to see if their predictions were accurate.

Segments That Are Enacted on the Spot

Lesson segments that are enacted on the spot involve classroom strategies and behaviors that might not be part of every lesson. However, when they are called for, a teacher must attend to them immediately, or the learning environment will quickly erode. Another way to conceptualize segments that are enacted on the spot is that they involve strategies that teachers must be prepared to use at a moment's notice even though the teacher has not necessarily planned to use them in a given lesson. Four types of segments fit into this general category: (1) increasing student engagement, (2) recognizing and acknowledging adherence or lack of adherence to classroom rules and procedures, (3) establishing and maintaining effective relationships with students, and (4) communicating high expectations for every student. These segments represent Design Questions 5, 7, 8, and 9, respectively.

Increasing Student Engagement

Strategies and behaviors to increase student engagement might be called for at any point during a lesson. Effective teachers continuously scan their classrooms to determine if students are engaged and take steps to reengage students if they are not. This type of lesson segment draws heavily from the research on student attention (Connell, Spencer, & Aber, 1994; Connell & Wellborn, 1991; Reeve, 2006). Specific strategies and behaviors associated with increasing student engagement include the following:

- Noticing and reacting when students are not engaged (e.g., the teacher scans the classroom to monitor students' level of engagement)
- Using academic games (e.g., when students are not engaged, the teacher uses adaptations of popular games to reengage them and focus their attention on academic content)
- Managing response rates during questioning (e.g., the teacher uses strategies such as response cards, response chaining, and voting technologies to ensure that multiple students respond to questions)
- Using physical movement (e.g., the teacher uses strategies that require students to move physically, such as vote with your feet and physical reenactments of content)
- Maintaining a lively pace (e.g., the teacher slows and quickens the pace of instruction in such a way as to enhance engagement)
- Demonstrating intensity and enthusiasm (e.g., the teacher uses verbal and nonverbal signals that he or she is enthusiastic about the content)
- Using friendly controversy (e.g., the teacher uses techniques that require students to take and defend a position about content)
- Providing opportunities for students to talk about themselves (e.g., the teacher uses techniques that allow students to relate content to their personal lives and interests)

• Presenting unusual or intriguing information (e.g., the teacher provides or encourages the identification of intriguing information about the content)

To illustrate how these strategies and behaviors might manifest in the classroom, consider a civics teacher who notices that his students are not paying adequate attention to his presentation on the rights and responsibilities of being a citizen. Noting students' apparent boredom, the teacher engages them in a brief physical activity that helps increase their energy, thus increasing engagement. Alternatively, the teacher might ask questions that require students to answer using response cards, thus ensuring that all students are engaged in responding to each question.

Recognizing and Acknowledging Adherence or Lack of Adherence to Classroom Rules and Procedures

Strategies and behaviors that acknowledge students' adherence to rules and procedures and lack of adherence to rules and procedures may be required at any point in a lesson. The strategies and behaviors for this type of segment draw from the general research on classroom management (Wang, Haertel, & Walberg, 1993) and discipline (Marzano et al., 2003). Specific strategies and behaviors associated with this type of segment include the following:

• Demonstrating "withitness" (e.g., the teacher is aware of variations in student behavior that might indicate potential disruptions and attends to them immediately)

• Applying consequences (e.g., the teacher applies consequences for lack of adherence to rules and procedures consistently and fairly)

• Acknowledging adherence to rules and procedures (e.g., the teacher acknowledges adherence to rules and procedures consistently and fairly)

To illustrate how these strategies and behaviors might manifest, consider an elementary physical education teacher who notices that students are not following the procedure for putting away equipment after a game of volleyball. The teacher points this out to students and takes some time to briefly review the procedure. On another occasion, the teacher notices that students have done a particularly good job at following the procedure for taking turns while practicing hitting a baseball off a tee. Again, the teacher points this out to students, noting how smoothly the class went and thanking students for their efforts.

Establishing and Maintaining Effective Relationships with Students

Effective teacher–student relationships are perhaps the keystone of teaching. If sound relationships exist between teacher and students, classroom activities progress more smoothly. Strategies and behaviors that address teacher–student relationships are drawn from the research regarding the need for a balance between student perceptions that the teacher is in control of the classroom and student perceptions that the teacher is their advocate (Brekelmans, Wubbels, & Creton, 1990; Wubbels, Brekelmans, den Brok, & van Tartwijk, 2006). Specific strategies and behaviors associated with segments devoted to enhancing teacher–student relationships include the following:

- Understanding students' interests and backgrounds (e.g., the teacher seeks out knowledge about students and uses that knowledge to engage in informal, friendly discussions with students)
- Using behaviors that indicate affection for students (e.g., the teacher uses humor and friendly banter appropriately with students)
- Displaying objectivity and control (e.g., the teacher behaves in ways that indicate he or she does not take infractions personally)

To illustrate how these strategies and behaviors might manifest, consider a high school mathematics teacher who notices that while students recognize that he is clearly in control, there is little levity in his classroom. Additionally, students seem reluctant to approach him regarding problems they are having with the content. To establish more balance in student perceptions, the teacher decides to lighten up the classroom atmosphere by using humor and some good-natured banter with students.

Communicating High Expectations for Students

The realm of teacher expectations deals with the phenomenon that teachers form expectations for individual students relatively quickly. For some students, teachers develop high expectations; for other students, they develop low expectations. Unfortunately, teachers tend to treat high-expectation and low-expectation students differently. Students quickly recognize behavioral clues that they are expected to do well or poorly academically and then behave accordingly (Rosenthal & Jacobson, 1968). Strategies and behaviors regarding expectations draw from the research on establishing an appropriate affective tone with all students and providing equal opportunities to all students for complex academic interactions (Weinstein, 2002). Specific strategies and behaviors associated with segments devoted to communicating high expectations include the following:

- Demonstrating value and respect for low-expectancy students (e.g., the teacher demonstrates the same positive affective tone with low-expectancy students as with high-expectancy students)
- Asking questions of low-expectancy students (e.g., the teacher asks questions of low-expectancy students with the same frequency and level of difficulty as with high-expectancy students)

- Probing incorrect answers with low-expectancy students (e.g., the teacher inquires into incorrect answers with low-expectancy students with the same depth and rigor as with high-expectancy students)

To illustrate how these strategies and behaviors might manifest in the classroom, consider a high school AP calculus teacher who realizes that she asks questions almost exclusively of students who voluntarily participate in class. In contrast, she does not call on specific students who appear to be struggling, to avoid embarrassing them or making them feel uncomfortable. She institutes a policy of asking difficult questions of every student. Although this change in her behavior is challenging to some students at first, over time, they accept the fact that all students are expected to address complex content, and their thinking will be respected even if it has some flaws in it.

Summary of Domain 1

Domain 1 addresses classroom strategies and behaviors that have a direct effect on student achievement. These are organized into three broad categories of lesson segments: routine segments, content segments, and segments that are enacted on the spot. Within these three general categories of segments are embedded 41 types of instructional strategies and behaviors from the first nine design questions of *The Art and Science of Teaching* (Marzano, 2007).

Domain 2: Planning and Preparing

As indicated in Figure 3.2, *The Art and Science of Teaching* (Marzano, 2007) involves 10 design questions. The first nine of these questions and their related strategies and behaviors constitute the totality of Domain 1. The 10th design question in Figure 3.2 deals with planning and preparing—the focus of Domain 2. In all, this domain involves three general categories of activities regarding planning and preparing: (1) lessons and units, (2) materials and resources, and (3) special needs of students.

Planning and Preparing for Lessons and Units

This category from Domain 2 focuses on planning and preparing for units of instruction and the lessons within those units. This type of planning and preparing draws on the research regarding the relationship between teacher planning and decision making and student achievement (Blumenfeld & Meece, 1988; Clark & Peterson, 1986; Doyle, 1983, 1986; Schoenfeld, 1998, 2006). Specific activities associated with this category are the following:

- Planning and preparing for effective scaffolding of information within lessons (e.g., within lessons, the teacher organizes content in such a way that each new piece of information builds on the previous piece)
- Planning and preparing for lessons within a unit that progress toward a deep understanding and transfer of content (e.g., the teacher organizes lessons within a unit so that students move from an understanding of the foundational content to applying that content in authentic ways)
- Planning and preparing for appropriate attention to established content standards (e.g., the teacher ensures that lessons and units include the important content identified by the district and the manner in which that content should be sequenced)

To illustrate how these activities might manifest, consider an elementary teacher in a district that has provided a pacing guide for her to follow. The pacing guide provides a significant amount of detail, but the teacher still has planning and preparing issues to address. As she develops her units and lessons within those units, she makes sure to include the "essential learnings" listed in the pacing guide as well as the manner in which these essential learnings are sequenced. Within each unit, she organizes her lessons in such a way that by the end of the unit, students are applying what they have learned through novel and ideally authentic activities. Within lessons in which new information is being presented, she makes sure that each new piece of information has a logical connection to the previous information that was presented and develops ways to highlight these connections.

Planning and Preparing for Use of Materials and Technology

This category focuses on the appropriate use of traditional materials such as books, videotapes, DVDs, manipulatives, and the like. It also addresses the appropriate use of technology when available. Traditional materials have always been an important part of effective teaching (Emmer et al., 1980; Evertson & Weinstein, 2006). Technologies such as interactive whiteboards and one-to-one computing are relatively new to K–12 education but hold the promise of dramatically changing teaching and learning (Newby, Stepich, Lehman, Russell, & Ottenbreit-Leftwich, 2011). The specific activities within this category are as follows:

- Planning and preparing for the use of available materials for upcoming units and lessons (e.g., the teacher identifies available traditional materials that can enhance students' understanding of the content in a given lesson or unit and determines how these materials might best be used)
- Planning and preparing for the use of available technologies such as interactive whiteboards, response systems, and computers (e.g., the teacher identifies

the available technologies that can enhance students' understanding of content in a given lesson or unit and decides how those technologies will be used)

To illustrate how these activities might manifest, consider a science teacher planning for a lesson on the concept of percolation—the process of filtering liquids through porous rock formations. The teacher identifies the pages in the textbook that will be used. Additionally, she finds some pictures from the Internet that will provide students with interesting images of the process of percolation. She also realizes that students might benefit greatly from a series of well-designed questions in which they record immediate feedback on their answers. She plans to use the voting technology that is a feature of the new interactive whiteboard that was purchased for her classroom.

Planning and Preparing for Special Needs of Students

Without question, the diversity of students within K–12 classrooms is expanding. According to the National Center for Education Statistics (nces.ed.gov), the percentage of students in the United States living at or below the poverty line has increased from 15.4 percent to 17.4 percent between 2000 and 2008; the percentage of English language learners (ELLs) has increased from 5.0 percent to 5.2 percent between 1999 and 2007; and the percentage of students with learning disabilities has increased from 11.4 percent to 13.6 percent between 1990 and 2007. Given these circumstances, planning and preparing must include careful consideration of students with special needs. This category involves the following activities:

• Planning and preparing for the needs of English language learners (e.g., the teacher identifies the adaptations that must be made for specific ELLs regarding a lesson or unit)

• Planning and preparing for the needs of special education students (e.g., the teacher identifies adaptations that must be made for specific special education students regarding a lesson or unit)

• Planning and preparing for the needs of students who come from home environments that offer little support for schooling (e.g., the teacher identifies adaptations that must be made for specific students who come from homes with few material and psychological resources)

To illustrate how these activities might manifest, consider an elementary teacher in a self-contained classroom who is planning a unit on writing a five-paragraph essay. She realizes that of the eight ELL students in her class, three are close to being bilingual in English and Spanish. She identifies specific activities during which she will have her bilingual ELL students work with her other ELL students. She also makes adaptations for two special education students who have been mainstreamed into her room. Specifically, she will make sure that the practice activities for those students are much more structured than they are for other students. Finally, she considers two students in her class whom she knows will have little help and very few resources at home for academic activities. Given this, she realizes that any homework she assigns will have to be structured in such a way that it requires no help from parents or guardians and no resources other than those provided to every student in class.

Summary of Domain 2

This domain addresses planning and preparing. These activities are assumed to be directly related to classroom strategies and behaviors. The better a teacher plans and prepares, the more effective are his or her choices of classroom strategies and behaviors. Three categories of activities were addressed: (1) planning and preparing for lessons and units, (2) planning and preparing for the use of materials and technology, and (3) planning and preparing for special needs of students.

Domain 3: Reflecting on Teaching

Reflecting on teaching addresses teachers' ability and willingness to examine their own teaching in a metacognitive and evaluative manner. This domain is hypothesized to have a direct effect on planning and preparing (Domain 2). Reflecting on teaching contains two categories of activities: (1) evaluating personal performance and (2) developing and implementing a professional growth plan.

Evaluating Personal Performance

Self-evaluation has long been considered an important aspect of personal growth (Ericsson, Charness, Feltovich, & Hoffman, 2006). It is also a necessary component of what was referred to as deliberate practice in Chapter 1 (Ericsson et al., 1993). A teacher who is able to evaluate his or her performance has taken a giant step on the road to expertise. This category involves the following activities:

• Identifying specific areas of pedagogical strength and weakness within Domain 1 (e.g., the teacher identifies specific strategies and behaviors on which to improve from routine lesson segments, content lesson segments, and segments that are enacted on the spot)

• Evaluating the effectiveness of individual lessons and units (e.g., the teacher determines how effective a lesson or unit of instruction was in terms of enhancing student achievement and identifies causes of success or failure)

• Evaluating the effectiveness of specific pedagogical strategies and behaviors across different categories of students (i.e., different socioeconomic groups, different ethnic groups) (e.g., the teacher determines the effectiveness of specific instructional techniques regarding the achievement of subgroups of students and identifies reasons for discrepancies)

To illustrate how these activities might manifest, consider a French teacher who reflects on a unit of instruction on common verb forms. Using pre- and post-test data, she makes a determination as to how effective the unit was in terms of students achieving the learning goal. She concludes that overall, the unit went well and attributes its general success to the fact that she had students track their progress on the learning goal for the unit. On further analysis of the test data, she notices that many of her students classified as eligible for free and reduced-price lunch did not do as well as other students. She attributes this to the fact that she assigned too much homework that required support from home. As a result of her analysis of this unit, she identifies specific changes she will make in her next unit.

Developing and Implementing a Professional Growth Plan

Ultimately, a teacher's self-evaluation must translate into systematic action. The vehicle for such action is a professional growth and development plan. There are two activities within this category:

• Developing a written growth and development plan (e.g., the teacher develops a written professional growth and development plan with milestones and time lines)
• Monitoring progress relative to the professional growth plan (e.g., the teacher charts his or her progress using established milestones and time lines)

To illustrate how these activities might manifest, consider a middle school teacher who has identified one classroom strategy regarding routines, one strategy regarding content, and one strategy that is enacted on the spot as areas of personal growth for the next year. She sets growth goals for each one of these strategies in a written professional growth and development plan. Throughout the year, the teacher monitors the extent to which she is accomplishing her growth goals by charting her progress on the identified instructional strategies and student achievement. Using this feedback, she periodically adjusts her professional growth and development plan.

Summary of Domain 3

This domain addresses teacher self-reflection and involves two categories of activities: evaluating personal performance, and developing and implementing a professional growth plan. This domain might be thought of as a metacognitive aspect of teacher growth and development.

Domain 4: Collegiality and Professionalism

This domain is not directly related to enhanced classroom strategies and behaviors. However, collegiality and professionalism are the context in which the other domains function. If a district or school has high levels of collegiality and professionalism, Domains 1, 2, and 3 are enhanced.

To one extent or another, collegiality and professionalism have been mentioned by a variety of researchers and theorists as a critical aspect of school effectiveness. In the book *What Works in Schools*, Marzano (2003) identified collegiality and professionalism as one of five critical variables that have a strong correlation with student achievement. Although they use different terminology and have somewhat different emphasis, Scheerens and Bosker (1997), Levine and Lezotte (1990), and Sammons (1999) have also attested to the importance of this domain. While collegiality and professionalism are thought of as a school characteristic, they are actually a function of individual teacher actions. That is, it is the responsibility of individual teachers and administrators to develop an atmosphere of collegiality and professionalism. This domain includes three categories of activities: (1) promoting a positive environment, (2) promoting exchange of ideas and strategies, and (3) promoting district and school development.

Promoting a Positive Environment

A positive environment refers to the manner in which teachers and administrators interact with one another. It does not necessarily mean that teachers have established close friendships in the school. In fact, evidence indicates that an emphasis on friendships within a school building might detract from student achievement (Friedkin & Slater, 1994). It does mean that teachers engage in specific activities that create a professional environment that fosters teachers' development. This category involves two activities:

• Promoting positive interactions about colleagues (e.g., the teacher interacts with other teachers in a positive manner and helps extinguish negative conversations about other teachers)

• Promoting positive interactions about students and parents (e.g., the teacher interacts with students and parents in a positive manner and helps extinguish negative conversations about students and parents)

To illustrate how these actions might manifest, consider a high school teacher who makes it a point not to complain about fellow teachers, students, or their parents. He simply considers such conversations unprofessional. Likewise, when he hears other teachers complain or speak badly about teachers, students, or parents, he tries to add a positive perspective on these individuals. In some cases, he even reminds those teachers who are complaining that it would be better if they expressed those frustrations at home as opposed to expressing them in school.

Promoting Exchange of Ideas and Strategies

The free and open exchange of ideas and strategies is a powerful tool in the development of expertise. Certainly one aspect of professionalism is the extent to which a teacher fosters such interchange. This notion is supported by much of the research on teacher collaboration and professional learning communities (PLCs) (DuFour, DuFour, Eaker, & Karhanek, 2004; DuFour & Eaker, 1998; DuFour, Eaker, & DuFour, 2005). The teacher leadership literature also makes mention of these activities (York-Barr & Duke, 2004). This category has two activities:

• Seeking mentorship for areas of need or interest (e.g., the teacher seeks help and input from colleagues regarding specific classroom strategies and behaviors)

• Mentoring other teachers and sharing ideas and strategies (e.g., the teacher provides other teachers with help and input regarding specific classroom strategies and behaviors)

To illustrate how these activities might manifest, consider a middle school teacher who is working on classroom strategies and behaviors that communicate high expectations for all students. He knows of another teacher in the building who is quite skilled in this area. He seeks her out and asks her about specific strategies and behaviors she uses. Additionally, when other teachers approach him about instructional strategies and behaviors, he readily shares ideas.

Promoting District and School Development

Ultimately, teacher collegiality and professionalism must translate into support for school and district initiatives. Again, this is mentioned regularly in the literature on teacher leadership (York-Barr & Duke, 2004). This category includes two activities:

• Adhering to district and school rules and procedures (e.g., the teacher is aware of the district's and school's rules and procedures and adheres to them)

• Participating in district and school initiatives (e.g., the teacher is aware of the district's and school's initiatives and participates in them in accordance with his or her talents and availability)

To illustrate how these activities might manifest, consider a teacher who, upon being hired into a new district, becomes familiar with the policies regarding teacher dress, teacher behavior, and so on. She wants to make sure that she follows all rules and regulations. Additionally, she inquires into the various outreach initiatives in which the district is involved. She knows she won't have much free time, but she wants to contribute to the best of her ability and availability.

Summary of Domain 4

Dealing with teacher collegiality and professional behavior, Domain 4 involves promoting a positive environment, promoting the exchange of ideas and strategies, and promoting district and school development. Although these behaviors are only indirectly related to the enhancement of classroom strategies and behaviors, they are still an important aspect of developing expertise in that they form the foundation on which the other three domains are developed.

Summary

This chapter addressed the knowledge base for teaching, which is foundational to systematically developing expertise. Four domains were described, along with the specific elements that constitute each. Domain 1 deals with classroom strategies and behaviors. It is the most detailed domain and is thought to have a direct relationship with student achievement. Domain 2 deals with planning and preparing and is believed to have a direct relationship with Domain 1. Domain 3, reflecting on teaching, is thought to have a direct relationship with Domain 2. Domain 4 addresses collegiality and professionalism and is considered the context in which the other three domains function.

CHAPTER 4

Focused Feedback and Practice

The four domains described in Chapter 3 provide a framework for teacher growth and development. If teachers systematically attend to classroom strategies and behaviors (Domain 1), planning and preparing (Domain 2), reflecting on teaching (Domain 3), and collegiality and professionalism (Domain 4), they will surely enhance their professional status. However, as shown in Figure 1.2, these domains are not independent. Rather, Domain 1 is the focal point in that it is most directly tied to student achievement. Consequently, improving a teacher's strategies and behaviors in the classrooam should be the primary focus of supervision and evaluation. To a great extent, activities in the other domains serve Domain 1. Domain 2 increases expertise in Domain 1, Domain 3 enhances expertise in Domain 2, and Domain 4 is the context in which the other three domains function. In short, given its importance, Domain 1 should be the subject of focused feedback and practice.

Levels of Performance

Focused feedback requires clear descriptions of levels of performance. Regarding classroom strategies and behaviors, this means articulating performance levels for the 41 elements within Domain 1. For purposes of illustration, we will use an element from lesson segments that involve content. Specifically, we will consider an element from content lesson segments whose purpose is to introduce new content. As depicted in Figure 3.1, eight elements are involved in this type of segment, one of which is the strategy of previewing the content.

Although previewing content is a fairly specific behavior, there are gradations to its effective use. That is, not every teacher who engages students in a previewing activity does it effectively. There are highly effective ways to preview new content, moderately effective ways to preview new content, and even relatively ineffective ways to preview new content. The proper role of focused feedback is to provide teachers with a sense of where they fall on such a continuum. To this end, each element for Domain 1 has an associated rubric or scale. These are scales reported in Appendix A. It is important to note that each scale for Domain 1 reported in Appendix A is embedded in an observational protocol. This protocol is explained later in this chapter. The scale for this particular element is shown in Figure 4.1.

| FIGURE 4.1 | Scale for Previewing New Content |

	Innovating (4)	Applying (3)	Developing (2)	Beginning (1)	Not Using (0)
Previewing New Content	Adapts and creates new strategies for unique student needs and situations.	Engages students in learning activities that require them to preview and link new knowledge to what has been addressed and monitors the extent to which students are making linkages.	Engages students in learning activities that require them to preview and link new knowledge to what has been addressed.	Uses strategy incorrectly or with parts missing.	Strategy was called for but not exhibited.

© 2011 Robert J. Marzano

The scale in Figure 4.1 has five values ranging from 0 to 4. The scale value of 0, or Not Using, indicates that the strategy is called for but not used by the teacher. That is, there are occasions when the strategy of previewing can and perhaps should be used, but the teacher does not employ the strategy on those occasions. The scale value of 1, Beginning, indicates that the teacher uses previewing strategies but does so with some errors. The scale value of 2, Developing, indicates that the teacher uses previewing strategies without any significant errors. The scale value of 3, Applying, is the minimum desired status for any element in Domain 1 (as well as the other three domains). Here the teacher engages students in previewing activities and monitors whether students are making linkages between the new content and their prior knowledge. At the Developing level, the teacher employs the strategy without error but does not check to see if it has the desired effect on students. At the Applying level, the teacher monitors student behavior and makes adaptations if necessary. Finally, a score value of 4, Innovating, indicates that the teacher is so skilled at previewing strategies that he or she has developed versions or adaptations of his or her own that meet specific needs of the class.

Every scale in Appendix A has the same syntax. Stated differently, every scale in Appendix A follows the same generic format depicted in Figure 4.2. In Figure 4.2, the descriptions for scale values Not Using (0), Beginning (1), and Innovating (4) are identical to the descriptions in Figure 4.1. For all 41 elements of Domain 1, scale values 0, 1, and 4 are the same. However, scale values 2 (Developing) and 3 (Applying) are specific to each element. This noted, Developing always means that a particular strategy is being used without significant errors or omissions. Applying always means not only that the strategy is used without error, but also that the teacher monitors whether the desired effect on students has been realized.

FIGURE 4.2	Generic Format of Scales for Domain 1

	Innovating (4)	Applying (3)	Developing (2)	Beginning (1)	Not Using (0)
Target Strategy	Adapts and creates new strategies for unique student needs and situations.	Engages students in the strategy and monitors the extent to which it produces the desired outcomes.	Engages students in the strategy with no significant errors or omissions.	Uses strategy incorrectly or with parts missing.	Strategy was called for but not exhibited.

© 2011 Robert J. Marzano

The scales in Appendix A stand in sharp contrast to some other vehicles currently used to provide teachers with feedback. Specifically, we have observed some feedback protocols in which classroom strategies and behaviors are simply "checked off" as being used or not used. In a scheme like that, instructional strategies and behaviors appear in a simple checklist. The only feedback teachers receive is whether they use the strategy. Such a process provides no feedback as to the level of skill a teacher exhibits relative to a particular strategy. This absence violates a basic principle of effective feedback; namely, it should provide teachers with clear direction regarding how to improve. Scales provide such guidance, checkmarks do not. In a 2009 article entitled "Setting the Record Straight on High Yield Strategies," Marzano warned about the misuses of simple checklist approaches to providing feedback to teachers. Briefly, he noted that simply providing teachers with feedback that they either used a strategy or did not use a strategy does little to enhance teacher expertise.

In addition to scales for each element, Appendix A also contains examples of teacher evidence and student evidence of the use of specific strategies. The teacher and student evidence for the element of previewing new content is provided in Figure 4.3. As the figure shows, teacher evidence for this element includes behaviors such as asking preview questions before reading, having students brainstorm, and the like. Student evidence includes behaviors such as "Students can explain linkages with prior knowledge" and "Students can make predictions about the content." It is important not to equate quantity of strategies with level of performance. For example, just because a given teacher exhibits multiple behaviors in Figure 4.3 does not mean that the teacher has reached an advanced level on the scale for this element. *Again, expertise is a function of how strategies are used, not how many strategies are used.*

FIGURE 4.3	Previewing New Content

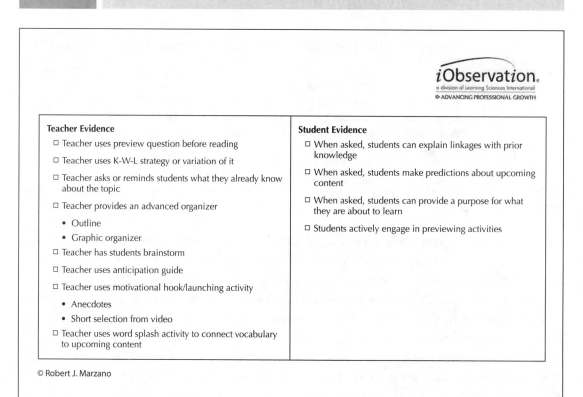

iObservation
a division of Learning Sciences International
▷ ADVANCING PROFESSIONAL GROWTH

Teacher Evidence
- ☐ Teacher uses preview question before reading
- ☐ Teacher uses K-W-L strategy or variation of it
- ☐ Teacher asks or reminds students what they already know about the topic
- ☐ Teacher provides an advanced organizer
  - Outline
  - Graphic organizer
- ☐ Teacher has students brainstorm
- ☐ Teacher uses anticipation guide
- ☐ Teacher uses motivational hook/launching activity
  - Anecdotes
  - Short selection from video
- ☐ Teacher uses word splash activity to connect vocabulary to upcoming content

Student Evidence
- ☐ When asked, students can explain linkages with prior knowledge
- ☐ When asked, students make predictions about upcoming content
- ☐ When asked, students can provide a purpose for what they are about to learn
- ☐ Students actively engage in previewing activities

© Robert J. Marzano

Providing Focused Feedback

The first step for any teacher who seeks to increase his or her pedagogical skills regarding the strategies and behaviors of Domain 1 is to identify and focus on specific areas of pedagogical strength and weakness. Focused feedback is a necessary tool to this end. There are a number of ways focused feedback can be provided regarding the 41 elements of Domain 1. Here we consider five ways to provide focused feedback: (1) teacher self-rating, (2) walkthroughs, (3) observations, (4) cueing teaching, and (5) student surveys.

Teacher Self-Rating

Teacher self-rating is one of the easiest and least threatening ways for teachers to obtain information on their performance regarding Domain 1. Teacher self-rating is not a new idea. Ross and Bruce (2007) discuss its use in their article "Teacher Self-Assessment: A Mechanism for Facilitating Professional Growth." They conclude that "providing a self-assessment tool is a constructive strategy for improving the effectiveness of in-service provided it is bundled with other professional growth strategies: peer coaching, observation by external change agents, and focused input on teaching strategies" (p. 146).

To collect self-rating data, teachers simply score themselves on each of the 41 elements in Domain 1 using the scales in the observational protocol in Appendix A. Simply stated, a teacher assigns him- or herself a score of Not Using (0) through Innovating (4) on each element. We have found that teachers are open to and even enthusiastic about this process as long as they know its purpose is to improve their pedagogical skills.

In addition to or in lieu of self-perception data, teachers can use videotapes of themselves to generate self-ratings. The use of video as a feedback mechanism has a rich history in K–12 education. For example, Rosaen, Lundeberg, Cooper, Fritzen, and Terpstra (2008) found that when teacher interns used video of their own teaching as the basis for reflection as compared to recollections, they were more likely to emphasize instructional components and "paid more attention to the children in terms of instruction, student achievement, and listening to the students, thus moving the focus away from self and onto the children" (p. 353). One subject in the study concluded that her reflection without the video was based on a feeling of how the lesson went rather than the video-based evidence that required a more honest analysis. Furthermore, the ability to review a lesson multiple times, pause the video, and engage in focused reflection greatly added to professional growth.

In another study, King (2008) found that preservice teachers "overwhelmingly felt that a visual record of their teaching inspired them to reflect more critically"

(p. 28). Sewall (2009) found video-elicited reflection had a number of positive effects over traditional approaches. When a lesson was observed by a supervisor and followed with a postconference, teachers talked less and were less reflective during the postconference than when engaged in a video-based reflection. Furthermore, the dialogue and the reflection were dominated by the supervisor. Teachers were relegated to a defensive position, sometimes haggling over what had actually happened during the lesson rather than reflecting on the lesson itself. This outcome was in stark contrast to the video-elicited reflection in which teachers spoke more frequently than their supervisors and offered deeper levels of analysis and reflection.

Finally, Calandra, Brantley-Dias, Lee, and Fox (2009) asked novice teachers to engage in two different methods of postlesson analysis. Each member of the control group debriefed with a teacher educator after his or her lesson and later wrote about two critical incidents from that lesson. Members of the experimental group recorded and reviewed their lesson on video and edited the video to present two critical incidents. After the editing was completed, the experimental group was also asked to write about the two critical incidents. Novice teachers in the experimental group produced longer reflections, were more likely to connect student behaviors to their own pedagogy, and were more likely to describe "transformations in their thinking about teaching" (p. 81).

Teacher self-rating using videotape is a fairly straightforward process. Teachers videotape a typical lesson and then at their leisure score themselves on the 41 elements in Appendix A. We recommend that when scoring their videotapes, teachers view them multiple times for various aspects of Domain 1. For example, during the first viewing, a teacher might focus on the use of routines. During the second viewing, the teacher might identify the content lesson segment that was being employed and analyze behaviors relative to that category of segment. During the third viewing, the teacher would examine the use of strategies that are enacted on the spot. There will most probably be elements of Domain 1 that were not observable in the video segment. For example, if the taped lesson focused on a content segment involving new knowledge, the teacher would not be able to observe him- or herself using strategies or behaviors that address practicing and deepening knowledge or applying knowledge by generating and testing hypotheses. For these unobserved elements, the teacher would simply score him- or herself based on perceptions of general behavior.

Walkthroughs

Walkthroughs have gained in prominence since the publication of the book *The Three-Minute Classroom Walk-through: Changing School Supervisory Practice One Teacher at a Time* by Carolyn Downey and her colleagues (Downey, Steffy,

English, Frase, & Posten, 2004). The authors characterized the philosophy of walkthroughs as follows:

> The Downey approach to classroom walk-throughs . . . rejects the superior-subordinate hegemony of principals and teachers that is often swathed in covert gender discrimination and replaces it with a collegial, egalitarian model of professional practice. It is centered on an adult-to-adult model of discourse that involves professional conversation about practice. (p. ix)

Defining characteristics of the Downey walkthrough approach include:

1. Short, focused, yet informal observation.

2. Possible area for teacher reflection.

3. Follow-up occurs only on occasion and not after each visit.

4. There is no checklist of things to look for or judgments to be made. Checklists signal a formal observation and one that often looks like an inspection to the teacher. (Downey et al., 2004, pp. 3–4)

The reasons cited for conducting walkthroughs are many: frequent observations of teachers lower their apprehension, making formal observations more effective; the more supervisors and instructional coaches are in the classroom, the more they know about the school's operations; and frequent walkthroughs allow for the identification of patterns of instructional practices in a school.

When conducting walkthroughs (or any other type of observation) using the protocol in Appendix A, it is imperative that observers identify a specific type of segment on which to initially focus. Consequently, a question that is continually being asked by observers engaged in walkthroughs is "What am I observing right now?" Subordinate questions to this inquiry are as follows:

- Is it a segment that involves routines? If so, what type of routine?
- Is it a segment that involves content? If so, what type of content segment is it?
- Is it a segment that involves on-the-spot activities? If so, what type of activity?

To illustrate, while conducting walkthroughs on a given day, an observer might enter a classroom and initially note that content is being addressed. In other words, the observer's answer to the question "What am I observing right now?" is that the teacher is engaged in a content lesson segment. More specifically, the observer would note that a content segment that involves deepening and practicing knowledge is being enacted. As we saw in Chapter 2, this type of segment involves the following teacher behaviors and student behaviors:

- Reviewing content (e.g., the teacher briefly reviews related content addressed previously)
- Organizing students to practice and deepen knowledge (e.g., the teacher organizes students into groups designed to review information or practice skills)
- Using homework (e.g., the teacher uses homework for independent practice or to elaborate on information)
- Examining similarities and differences (e.g., the teacher engages students in comparing, classifying, and creating analogies and metaphors)
- Examining errors in reasoning (e.g., the teacher asks students to examine informal fallacies, propaganda, and bias)
- Practicing skills, strategies, and processes (the teacher uses massed and distributed practice)
- Revising knowledge (e.g., the teacher asks students to revise entries in notebooks to clarify and add to previous information)

Of these strategies, the observer might note that the students are being asked to revise the entries in their academic notebooks. As a secondary focus, the observer might also note that the teacher reminds students of the goals for the unit. This is one of the routine behaviors that should be a systematic part of most, if not all, lessons. Finally, the observer might also notice that the teacher acknowledges that students are following a specific rule or procedure. This is one of the behaviors teachers should be prepared to address on the spot as they occur. Thus, even though the walkthrough lasted only three to five minutes, the administrator was able to observe behaviors from each of the three general types of lesson segments: a content segment in which students were practicing and deepening their knowledge, a routine segment in which students were being reminded of instructional goals, and an on-the-spot segment in which students were being acknowledged for following a rule or procedure.

When first becoming familiar with observational protocol for Domain 1, some observers prefer to begin with an abbreviated form such as that in Appendix B. We refer to this as the short form (as opposed to the long form in Appendix A). Figure 4.4 reports the elements from lesson segments involving routine events.

Notice that the short form does not include any teacher evidence or student evidence. It simply lists and describes each of the 41 elements and provides a place to take notes and/or assign a rating (i.e., I = Innovation, A = Applying, D = Developing, B = Beginning, and NU = Not Using).

In working with districts and schools, we have found that some observers prefer an even simpler form than the short form. Specifically, they begin with the snapshot form that is found in Appendix C. Figure 4.5 reports the section of the snapshot form that addresses routine events.

FIGURE 4.4	Elements for Routines: Short Form

Design Question 1: What will I do to establish and communicate learning goals, track student progress, and celebrate success?

1. Providing clear learning goals and scales to measure those goals (e.g., the teacher provides or reminds students about a specific learning goal)	Notes						
			I (4)	A (3)	D (2)	B (1)	NU (0)
2. Tracking student progress (e.g., using formative assessment, the teacher helps students chart their individual and group progress on a learning goal)	Notes						
			I (4)	A (3)	D (2)	B (1)	NU (0)
3. Celebrating student success (e.g., the teacher helps students acknowledge and celebrate current status on a learning goal as well as knowledge gain)	Notes						
			I (4)	A (3)	D (2)	B (1)	NU (0)

Design Question 6: What will I do to establish and maintain classroom rules and procedures?

4. Establishing classroom routines (e.g., the teacher reminds students of a rule or procedure or establishes a new rule or procedure)	Notes						
			I (4)	A (3)	D (2)	B (1)	NU (0)
5. Organizing the physical layout of the classroom for learning (e.g., the teacher organizes materials, traffic patterns, and displays to enhance learning)	Notes						
			I (4)	A (3)	D (2)	B (1)	NU (0)

FIGURE 4.5	Elements for Routines: Snapshot Form

Lesson Segments That Involve Routine Events That Might Be Observed in Every Lesson

• What is the teacher doing to help establish and communicate learning goals, track student progress, and celebrate success?

• What is the teacher doing to establish or maintain classroom rules and procedures?

With the snapshot form, no specific elements are listed—only the design questions that relate to routines. An observer simply records notes regarding what occurred throughout the walkthrough.

One useful convention to follow when conducting a walkthrough is for observers to make a brief scan of the observation form immediately after the walkthrough is conducted. For example, after observing a teacher during the three- to five-minute walkthrough, during which specific strategies and behaviors were recorded, the observer would briefly scan through the 41 elements in Appendix A that were not initially observed during the walkthrough. This might remind the observer of a strategy or behavior that occurred but was not recorded. For example, while reviewing the form, the observer might remember that the teacher exhibited behaviors that forged positive relationships with students even though such behaviors were not recorded during the walkthrough.

Data from walkthroughs can be used for two purposes. One is feedback to individual teachers. To provide this, teachers who had been observed during walkthroughs would receive a report identifying the strategies and behaviors that were observed. It is important to keep in mind that the absence of strategies and behaviors being observed does not necessarily imply anything negative about the teacher being observed. It might simply be the case that a given strategy or behavior was not appropriate during the interval of time during which the walkthrough occurred. This is particularly true with walkthroughs. Because they last for such a short time (e.g., three to five minutes), it would be impossible to observe all 41 elements of Domain 1.

Perhaps the most difficult aspect of a walkthrough is the rating on the scales that have been developed for each of the 41 elements in Domain 1 (see Appendix A). Recall that these scales have five values ranging from Not Using (0) to Innovating (4). These scales do not have to be used to provide feedback to teachers. In fact, in our experience, many teachers prefer anecdotal feedback to numeric ratings, particularly when walkthroughs are being conducted. In fact, hastily assigned numeric ratings can be quite unfair and counterproductive. City, Elmore, Fiarman, and Teitel (2009) allude to the dangers of hasty judgments about teacher performance:

> Unfortunately, the practice of walkthroughs has become corrupted in many ways by confounding it with supervision and evaluation of teachers. The purpose of some walkthroughs has been to identify deficiencies in classroom practice and to "fix" teachers who manifest these deficiencies. In many instances, judgments about what needs fixing are made on the basis of simplistic checklists that have little or nothing to do with direct experience of teachers in their classrooms. Groups of administrators descend on classrooms

with clipboards and checklists, caucus briefly in the hallway, and then deliver a set of simplistic messages about what needs fixing. This kind of practice is antithetical to the purposes of instructional rounds and profoundly anti-professional. (p. 4)

To avoid the problems associated with hasty numeric ratings assigned during walkthroughs, we suggest that observers rely primarily on anecdotal feedback during walkthroughs. For example, an observer might note that a teacher is using a specific previewing strategy. Additionally, the observer might note that the teacher completes the strategy, but does not seem to monitor to see if the strategy is actually helping students activate their prior knowledge relative to the topic being studied. This would equate to a score of Developing (2) on the scale for this element. Rather than simply reporting to the teacher that his or her score is a 2 or Developing, a statement like the following might be presented to the teacher in written or e-mail form: "I saw that you were having students preview the chapter in the book before they read it. How well do you think this helped students activate their prior knowledge of the topic?"

If numeric ratings are to be assigned during walkthroughs, we recommend that teachers should be asked to provide their own ratings for the elements observed. After a walkthrough, an observer might provide one numeric rating while the teacher provides a different numeric rating on a given element. For example, regarding a particular element, an observer might assign a rating of Beginning (1), whereas the teacher assigns himself a rating of Developing (2). The teacher would then be asked to justify his self-rating. In this case, the teacher might explain that he is trying to adapt the strategy in question to the needs of this particular class. This is why he appeared to omit aspects of the strategy. Had he not been trying to adapt the strategy, no elements would have been omitted.

A second and perhaps more valid use of walkthroughs is to provide aggregate data for the entire faculty in a school. In these cases, the purpose of walkthroughs is not to provide feedback to individual teachers but to identify instructional patterns across a group of teachers. This is depicted in Figure 4.6, which reports frequencies of observed incidents across the 41 elements of Domain 1. In this case, multiple walkthroughs had been conducted in a particular school, producing the frequency data reported in Figure 4.6. The boldface number in parentheses indicates the number of times a particular element was observed. Notice that the most frequently observed element addressed applying consequences for lack of adherence to rules and procedures. There were 23 observations of this behavior. Additionally, there were no observations of three strategies: reflecting on learning, examining errors in reasoning, and engaging students in tasks that require hypothesis generation and testing.

FIGURE 4.6	Aggregated Data from Walkthroughs with Potential Problems of Practice Highlighted

Routine Segments

Design Question 1: What will I do to establish and communicate learning goals, track student progress, and celebrate success?

1. Providing clear learning goals and scales to measure those goals **(6)**
2. Tracking student progress **(7)**
3. Celebrating student success **(4)**

Design Question 6: What will I do to establish and maintain classroom rules and procedures?

4. Establishing classroom routines **(12)**
5. Organizing the physical layout of the classroom for learning **(13)**

Content Segments

Design Question 2: What will I do to help students effectively interact with new knowledge?

1. Identifying critical information **(5)**
2. Organizing students to interact with new knowledge **(12)**
3. Previewing new content **(15)**
4. Chunking content into "digestible bites" **(7)**
5. Group processing of new information **(12)**
6. Elaborating on new information **(11)**
7. Recording and representing knowledge **(11)**
8. **Reflecting on learning (0)**

Design Question 3: What will I do to help students practice and deepen their understanding of new knowledge?

9. Reviewing content **(9)**
10. Organizing students to practice and deepen knowledge **(10)**
11. Using homework **(6)**
12. Examining similarities and differences **(6)**
13. **Examining errors in reasoning (0)**
14. Practicing skills, strategies, and processes **(4)**
15. Revising knowledge **(2)**

Design Question 4: What will I do to help students generate and test hypotheses about new knowledge?

16. Organizing students for cognitively complex tasks **(5)**
17. **Engaging students in cognitively complex tasks involving hypothesis generating and testing (0)**
18. Providing resources and guidance **(8)**

Segments Enacted on the Spot

Design Question 5: What will I do to engage students?

1. Noticing and reacting when students are not engaged **(10)**
2. Using academic games **(5)**

3. Managing response rates during questioning **(9)**
4. Using physical movement **(3)**
5. Maintaining a lively pace **(5)**
6. Demonstrating intensity and enthusiasm **(8)**
7. Using friendly controversy **(2)**
8. Providing opportunities for students to talk about themselves **(1)**
9. Presenting unusual or intriguing information **(3)**

Design Question 7: What will I do to recognize and acknowledge adherence or lack of adherence to classroom rules and procedures?

10. Demonstrating "withitness" **(5)**
11. **Applying consequences (23)**
12. Acknowledging adherence to rules and procedures **(12)**

Design Question 8: What will I do to establish and maintain effective relationships with students?

13. Understanding students' interests and background **(3)**
14. Using behaviors that indicate affection for students **(6)**
15. Displaying objectivity and control **(5)**

Design Question 9: What will I do to communicate high expectations for all students?

16. Demonstrating value and respect for low-expectancy students **(3)**
17. Asking questions of low-expectancy students **(5)**
18. Probing incorrect answers with low-expectancy students **(3)**

This type of data allows for hypotheses about common instructional issues or problems that might exist. City and colleagues (2009) state that observational data should allow educators "to focus on a common problem of practice that cuts across all levels of the system" (p. 5). Data like that displayed in Figure 4.6 allows for such determination. For example, using the data in Figure 4.6, administrators and teachers in this school might hypothesize that behavior is an issue in the building since there were so many incidents of consequences being applied because students did not follow rules and procedures. They might also conclude that more attention should be paid to the three strategies for which no incidents were observed.

Comprehensive Observations

Comprehensive observations occur over an extended period of time—typically the majority of a class period and ideally an entire class period. Observations can be unannounced, but they are more effective if planned by the observer and the teacher being observed. Typically this involves a preconference where the observer and the teacher identify what will be the focus of the observation. For example, it might be determined that during the observation, the teacher will be conducting a lesson in which students are going to be practicing and deepening their knowledge (Design Question 3). The teacher might ask for specific feedback on how she conducts an activity involving similarities and differences—one of the elements common to this type of lesson segment. Additionally, the teacher might ask for feedback on the extent to which she communicates learning goals and helps students track their progress—both aspects of Design Question 1 that most commonly manifest as routine segments. Finally, the teacher might request feedback on the extent to which she stays aware of student engagement and makes adjustments as necessary. This is from Design Question 5 and is categorized as a type of lesson segment that is enacted on the spot. In short, the preconference is intended to set the stage for what will be the focus of the comprehensive observation.

When actually conducting the comprehensive observation, the attention of the observer is much more focused than during walkthroughs. Since the observer and the teacher have discussed the upcoming lesson, sections of the observational protocol that will be of most importance have already been identified, making data collection much more efficient. During the postconference, the teacher and observer meet to discuss the observed lesson. It is during these meetings that the scales in Appendix A can be used as powerful tools. The session might begin with the teacher being asked to rate herself in the specific elements that were observed. The observer would then share his ratings of the teacher on those same elements along with the anecdotal comments that had been recorded. Using the combined data, teacher and observer would work toward agreement regarding the teacher's rating in the elements observed.

Cueing Teaching

What we refer to as cueing teaching can be thought of as a special application of a comprehensive observation. Cueing teaching is used only with teachers who have such severe problems with one or more elements of Domain 1 that it renders their teaching ineffective. Typically, these elements come from (but are not limited to) Design Question 5 (engagement) and Design Question 7 (acknowledging adherence and lack of adherence to classroom rules and procedures). Both of these are types of lesson segments that are enacted on the spot. Additionally, both are key components of what is commonly referred to as classroom management (Marzano et al., 2003). A case can be made that if strategies for these two elements are not in place, a teacher will have little control of the classroom.

Cueing teaching begins with a preconference much like that conducted for a comprehensive observation. During the preconference, a specific strategy or behavior is identified as the focus of a cueing teaching session. To illustrate, assume that a teacher and supervisor identify "withitness" as the strategy that is to be the focus of cueing teaching. As indicated in Appendix A, withitness involves behaviors such as these:

- The teacher physically occupies all quadrants of the room.
- The teacher scans the entire room, making eye contact with all students.
- The teacher recognizes potential sources of disruption and deals with them immediately.
- The teacher proactively addresses inflammatory situations.

Together, the supervisor and teacher design cues that will be used to signal the teacher that some aspect of withitness should be executed. For example, the observer might hold up one finger to signal to the teacher that she should move about the room more. The observer might hold up two fingers to signal to the teacher that she should make more eye contact with students, and so on.

During the observation, the observer stations him- or herself at the back of the room where the students can't see the cues being displayed. Following the system agreed on during the preconference, the observer holds up various numbers of fingers to cue specific strategies and behaviors. As with a comprehensive observation, the teacher and observer meet for a postconference to discuss the observed lesson.

Student Surveys

A final type of data that can be used for feedback to teachers is student survey data. In Chapter 6, we consider how student survey data can be used as a measure of student achievement and engagement. Here we consider how student survey data can be used to provide feedback to teachers regarding classroom strategies and behaviors.

To illustrate, consider the sample survey questions in Figure 4.7. These questions provide teachers with direct feedback from students regarding Design Question 1, which is categorized as a routine behavior. Here students are asked to agree or disagree with statements that relate to how well the teacher uses strategies for communicating learning goals, tracking student progress, and celebrating success. Of course, to obtain valid information from students, their responses must be anonymous. At the end of a unit of instruction, a teacher might ask students to complete a survey like that in Figure 4.7 and then use the results as a form of feedback.

| FIGURE 4.7 | Sample Student Questions for Design Question 1 |

	I completely agree (4)	(3)	(2)	I completely disagree (1)
The learning goals for this class are clear to me.				
In this class, my teacher provides consistent feedback to me about my performance.				
I can use the feedback my teacher provides to me in this class, to help improve my performance.				
In this class I am asked to record and reflect on my progress toward learning goals.				
In this class my teacher notices when students do well.				

©2011 Robert J. Marzano

The Process of Focused Practice

With rich sources of feedback like those described in this chapter, teachers can engage in focused practice. As its name implies, focused practice aims at improvement in particular elements of Domain 1. Specifically, based on the feedback from teacher self-perception, walkthroughs, comprehensive observations, sessions involving cueing teaching, and student surveys, a teacher can select specific classroom strategies and behaviors that will be the focus of practice. For example, during a given quarter or trimester, a teacher might select the strategy of withitness as the subject of focused practice. During selected lessons, the teacher would try out specific techniques regarding withitness, with the goal of developing his competence relative to this strategy.

If the strategy is completely new to the teacher, he can expect to progress through at least three phases of development (Marzano, 1992). The first phase is referred to as the *cognitive phase*. During this phase, the teacher is attempting to understand the strategy, but not using it with any utility or effectiveness. Relative to the scales reported in Appendix A, the cognitive stage is aligned with the score value Not Using (0). At this level, a teacher might not feel comfortable actually using a strategy, simply because he is trying to understand it by reading about it or observing others using it. The second phase of skill development is the *shaping phase*. Here the teacher is experimenting with the strategy and trying different versions of it. This stage corresponds to score values Beginning (1) and Developing (2), during which the teacher moves from performing the strategy with some significant errors and omissions (Beginning) to eradicating the errors but still having to consciously think about the strategy to execute it (Developing). The third phase is referred to as the *autonomous phase*. During this phase, the teacher can perform the strategy with little conscious thought and can, therefore, attend to other issues while performing the strategy. This phase corresponds to score values Applying (3) and Innovating (4). At the level of Applying, the teacher can perform the strategy fluently and simultaneously monitor its effect on students. At the level of Innovating, the teacher can also make instantaneous adaptations that meet the needs of specific situations or specific students.

Focused practice involves a systematic progression through these three phases and the score values of the scales associated with them. The teacher tries the strategy or parts of the strategy in a few selected classes and then reflects on his current status using the scales in Appendix A. For example, after trying strategies for withitness for a week or so, the teacher might note that he has moved from Not Using to Beginning. The teacher would then plan what he will do to advance even further. He might determine that he would like to talk to some other teacher who has mastered the strategy to stimulate his thinking. To this end, it is useful if teachers graph their progress as depicted in Figure 4.8.

Notice that in Figure 4.8 the teacher has recorded five scores over a three-month period of time. The first score was a 1 (Beginning), indicating that the teacher knew enough about the strategy to try it, but her execution of the strategy involved some errors or omissions. Her final score was a 3 (Applying) indicating that the teacher performed the strategy fluently and could monitor the effect on students. As we explain in Chapter 6, these multiple scores can be produced by a combination of teacher self-report scores as well as scores from observers. Charting progress and recording personal reflections on growth relative to a strategy are at the core of focused practice.

FIGURE 4.8 **FIGURE 4.8**   Five Ratings Recorded Over Three Months for a Teacher

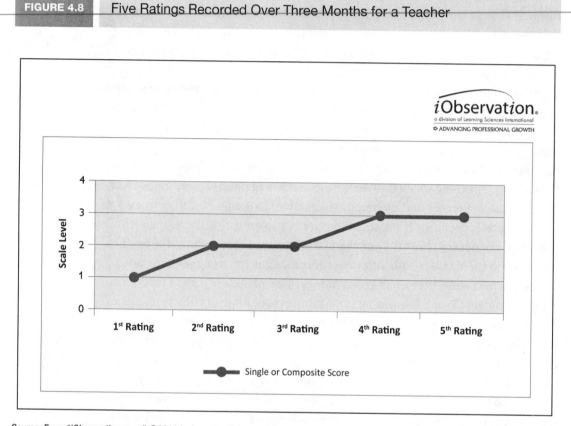

Summary

This chapter addressed focused feedback and practice—elements that are essential to developing expertise in Domain 1. Scales representing levels of performance on the 41 elements of Domain 1 were presented along with a discussion of the pitfalls of a checklist approach to providing teachers with feedback. Five ways to provide teacher feedback were described. Teacher self-rating is the least obtrusive form of feedback. Walkthroughs involve short visits to the classroom. Comprehensive observations involve a preconference, an observation, and a postconference. Cueing teaching is employed when a teacher needs focused feedback regarding specific strategies and behaviors. Student surveys gather information right from students regarding the use of classroom strategies and behaviors. With a wide variety of feedback options in place, teachers can engage in focused practice in which they chart their development in specific classroom strategies and behaviors.

CHAPTER 5

Opportunities to Observe and Discuss Expertise

As described in the previous chapter, learning a new strategy or behavior involves movement through phases. To effectively move through developmental phases, teachers must have opportunities to observe and discuss expertise. Simply stated, teachers need input from sources other than themselves. Unfortunately, the current K–12 education system in the United States is not well designed to meet this need. To the contrary, K–12 education has traditionally isolated teachers throughout their careers. Many researchers and theorists have commented on this phenomenon over the years. For example, Lieberman and Rosenholtz (1987) note:

> Most school people have learned to rely solely on themselves and their own experimental learning. What they learn is idiosyncratic. Isolation and insulation are the expected conditions in too many schools. These conditions do not foster individual teacher growth and school improvement. (p. 94)

Sagor (1992) cites the work of Roland Barth to dramatize the isolation of teachers:

> Teachers work in a different world. Roland Barth likened American teachers to a group of preschoolers engaged in parallel play. Although they may work in a building with other teachers and even use the same materials and follow the

same schedule, they rarely turn to one another during the school day except during their thirty-minute lunch period, where informal norms often forbid any kind of professional talk. This dearth of collegial stimulation would be bad enough if teaching were a profession with a certain and finite knowledge base. But the problems of teaching are ever changing, and absolute solutions are usually not to be found. Successful teaching is a mixture of art and craft honed through experience. In such a profession, a lack of meaningful discourse with fellow professionals can have disastrous effects. (p. 2)

Interestingly, collaboration and exchange of strategies and ideas appear to be highly valued in other professions as a concrete way to enhance the skills of all those within the profession. Gawande (2009) has chronicled the importance of collegial dialogue and shared practices in the medical profession. He notes that when doctors share their expertise, they produce more thinking and less superfluous testing. According to Gawande, the net effect of opportunities to discuss and observe effective practices within the medical profession is lowered costs and better patient care.

In *The Wisdom of Crowds*, Surowiecki (2004) reports on a 1966 study of 592 scientists and their collaborative activities. That study found that the most prolific scientist in terms of publications was by far the most collaborative, and three of the four next most prolific scientists were among the next most collaborative. Reporting on another study of 41 Nobel laureates, Surowiecki notes that laureates collaborated more than other scientists. While the study concedes the fact that it is easier for well-known scientists to collaborate because everyone wants to work with them: "the fact that they are committed to working with others when you might expect them to assume that they have nothing to gain from it, testifies to the centrality of cooperative effects in modern science" (p. 163).

A study conducted by Jackson and Bruegmann (2009) provides an interesting perspective on teachers learning from other teachers. Using data on 3rd grade through 5th grade students in North Carolina from 1995 to 2006, they were able to statistically estimate the effect on students' achievement of their teachers working with competent peers. They explain their findings in the following way:

The cumulative effect over three years of having peers with one standard deviation higher effectiveness is 0.078 standard deviations in math and 0.072 standard deviations in reading. Because teachers have about three peers on average, this is about one third of the size of the own-teacher effect, suggesting that over time, teacher peer quality is very important. Lastly, we find that peer quality in the previous two years "explains away" about one fifth of the explanatory power of individual teachers. This suggests that a sizable part of the own-teacher effect is learned as a result of exposure to her previous peers. Although we acknowledge that we cannot prove peer related learning, we believe these pieces of evidence lend themselves most naturally to a peer related learning interpretation (either learning directly from peers, or peer induced learning. (pp. 22–23)

In this chapter, we address five ways that teachers might observe and discuss effective teaching: (1) instructional rounds, (2) expert coaches, (3) expert videos, (4) teacher-led professional development, and (5) virtual communities.

Instructional Rounds

Instructional rounds are gaining popularity in K–12 education. The book *Instructional Rounds* by City and her colleagues (2009) describes the history and nature of rounds:

> The rounds process is an adaptation and extension of the medical rounds model, which is used routinely in medical schools and teaching hospitals to develop the diagnostic and treatment practice of physicians. There are several versions of medical rounds, but in the most commonly used versions, groups of medical interns, residents, and supervisory or attending physicians visit patients, observe and discuss the evidence for diagnoses, and, after a thorough analysis of the evidence, discuss possible treatments. The medical rounds process is the major way in which physicians develop their knowledge of practice and, more importantly, the major way in which the profession builds and propagates its forms of practice. (p. 3)

City and colleagues provide a caution regarding rounds that we share wholeheartedly:

> [R]ounds in and of themselves will not raise student scores and will not help districts make adequate yearly progress to meet the provisions of the No Child Left Behind legislation. If rounds is going to lead to changes in teaching and learning, it cannot be another initiative, activity, or program imposed on superintendents, principals, and teachers. The power of rounds will only be realized when and if rounds becomes embedded in the actual work of the district. Only if rounds develops a collaborative, inquiry-based culture that shatters the norms of isolation and autonomy and if it leads to the establishment of an "educational practice" that trumps the notion of teaching as an art, a craft, or a style will rounds transform teaching and learning. (p. xi)

In our model, rounds are one of the primary ways for teachers to observe and discuss effective teaching. It is important to note that our treatment of rounds is different from that of City et al. (2009). Where they focus on administrators conducting rounds, we focus on teachers conducting rounds.

During instructional rounds, small groups of teachers make relatively brief observations of their fellow teachers. These observations are longer than a typical walkthrough (i.e., longer than a few minutes) but usually shorter than an entire class period. When engaged in rounds, groups of teachers have as many substantive observations of classrooms as possible within part of a day or the entire day. For example, a group of teachers might spend an entire morning conducting three rounds and then discuss their experiences in the afternoon. Another option is to discuss experiences immediately after each observation.

The Function of Instructional Rounds

Instructional rounds are typically not used to provide feedback to the teacher being observed, although this is an option if the observed teacher so desires. The primary purpose of instructional rounds within our model is for the teachers making the observations to compare their practices with those observed in the classrooms they visit. It is the discussion at the end of a set of instructional rounds and the subsequent self-reflection by observer teachers that is their chief benefit.

We advocate that every teacher should have a chance to participate in instructional rounds at least once per year and, ideally, once per semester. Rounds are typically facilitated by a lead teacher—someone who is respected by their colleagues as an exceptional teacher and recognized as a professional. Instructional coaches commonly fit these characteristics. Administrators may also lead rounds, but it should be made clear from the outset that their purpose is not to evaluate the teachers being observed.

Teachers who are observed are typically volunteers. Ideally, these volunteers are drawn from the pool of veteran teachers in a district—those teachers who have proven their ability to enhance the achievement of all students in their classes. This noted, any teacher might offer his or her classroom as a venue for rounds.

Groups conducting rounds are usually small—three to five, not counting the lead teachers. On the day on which rounds are scheduled, teachers being observed alert their classes that they will have some other teachers visiting their classroom. Observed teachers might explain to their students that teachers in the building are trying to learn from one another just as students learn from one another.

When the observer teachers enter a classroom, they knock at the door and quietly move to some portion of the classroom that does not disrupt the flow of instruction. This is usually somewhere at the back of the classroom. There they observe what is occurring and make notes on what they see. At the end of the observation, the observer team exits the classroom making sure to thank the observed teacher and the students.

Debriefing Rounds

After rounds have been conducted, members of the observing team convene to debrief on their experiences, discussing each observation one at a time. This can be done in a round robin format where each observer teacher comments on what he or she noted. The leader of the rounds facilitates this process. The leader starts by reminding everyone that the purpose of the discussion is not to evaluate the observed teacher. Rules regarding how to share observations should be established prior to the debriefing. Useful rules include the following:

- Comments made during the debriefing should not be shared with anyone.
- Do not offer suggestions to the observed teachers unless they explicitly ask for feedback.
- Nothing observed within a lesson should be shared with anyone.
- Observed teachers should be thanked and acknowledged for their willingness to open their classrooms to others.

As observer teachers take turns commenting on what they saw in a particular classroom, it is useful to use a "pluses" and "deltas" format. The observer teacher begins by noting the positive things he or she observed in the classroom. Next the observer can mention some questions (deltas) he or she had about the teacher's use of strategies. Finally, the observer teacher compares and contrasts his or her classroom strategies with one or more or the techniques observed.

This process is completed for each classroom observed. For any particular observation, an observer teacher can opt not to share his or her analysis with the group. The debriefing ends with all observer teachers identifying one thing they might do differently in their classroom as a result of the rounds.

Expert Coaches

Under a different nomenclature, expert coaching has been a part of teacher development for decades. By the time of the publication of the October 1982 issue of *Educational Leadership*, the then recent research done by Bruce Joyce and Beverly Showers had penetrated deeply enough into the profession to command an entire issue entitled "The Coaching of Teaching." Joyce and Showers's (1982) article of the same title in that issue summarized their research on what it took to embed a new teaching skill deeply enough into a teacher's "active repertoire" for it to be used "regularly and sensibly" (p. 5). The authors' coaching language in this context is instructive: "coaching one another as they work the new model into their repertoire, providing companionship, helping each other learn to teach the appropriate responses to their students, figuring out the optimal uses of the model in their courses, and providing one another with ideas and feedback" (p. 5). It is clear from this statement and Joyce and Showers's article as a whole that coaching is best understood to be *peer* coaching, ideally with "coaching teams" developed during the training that precedes practice (p. 6).

In this same issue of *Educational Leadership*, editor Ron Brandt interviewed David Berliner regarding his perspective on improving teacher effectiveness. When Brandt asked, "Are you suggesting that principals and central office supervisors should concentrate their staff development efforts on in-class coaching?" Berliner's reply could not have been clearer: "I sure am. I think they should bring in fewer speakers and instead have somebody in classrooms helping teachers make changes" (Berliner, 1982, p. 14).

In the almost three decades since Joyce and Showers's influential writing on peer coaching, some useful distinctions have been drawn among coaching, consulting, and mentoring. For Garmston and Wellman (1999), *coaching* is facilitating the efforts of another as they move toward a goal. *Consulting* involves having your expertise used by others. It is in the consultative role that a colleague can provide technical knowledge, advocate for the use of a particular instructional strategy, or serve as a process advocate to guide a more effective implementation of an instructional strategy. Finally, *mentoring* is often understood to be the building of a one-to-one relationship for the purpose of providing guidance by a more experienced colleague for a beginning colleague (Levinson, 1977, cited in Glickman, 1985, p. 48). Although the distinctions sometimes blur, mentoring is usually less technical in its scope and more global in its purpose than coaching and consulting. But whatever terms are used, Sarason (1996) notes that when a young teacher is provided an "evaluation-free relationship" with a more masterful colleague, there is an increased chance that the inexperienced teacher will grow in skillfulness and effectiveness (p. 211).

Paralleling the decades-long interest in coaching, consulting, and mentoring are similar discussions in the general management literature. As an example, in *Influencer: The Power to Change Anything*, the authors write:

Perhaps the most obvious condition that demands social support as a means of influencing vital behaviors comes with the need for feedback that can be offered only by a pair of outside eyes. Anyone who has ever tried to learn tennis on his or her own and then gone head-on with someone who has spent a similar amount of time practicing with the aid of a coach quickly learns that real-time feedback from an expert beats solo practice any day. This being the case, you'd think that most people would turn to coaches to help in key areas of their lives, but they don't. Only a few ask for feedback outside of sports arenas. (Patterson, Grenny, Maxfield, McMillan, & Switzler, 2008, p. 188)

As previously defined, coaching has been done by peers, and consulting and mentoring by educators thought to be expert. In our model, coaching is more closely aligned with previous uses of the terms *consulting* and *mentoring*. For us, coaching should be done by expert teachers as opposed to peers. This is because those teachers being coached are seeking expert advice on specific classroom strategies and behaviors. Peers might not be able to provide the appropriate level of feedback. Coaches, then, must have the credentials traditionally held by mentors. However, whereas the mentor's role was more general in nature, coaching within our system requires specific technical feedback. The function of expert coaches within our approach also has a consultative orientation in that coaches seek to pass on their expertise to other teachers.

Expert coaches should be identified at the district level. In Chapter 7, we consider specific criteria that might be used for these selections. These experts would have a variety of functions within a district including: leading instructional rounds, leading sessions involving cueing teaching, conducting professional development workshops, and being the subject of expert videos. At a grassroots level, versions of these functions are already occurring. For example, Semadeni (2010) describes a coalition of schools in Wyoming that focuses on teachers identifying specific instructional strategies they wish to work on over a given period of time. Some teachers become "teacher experts" on specific strategies: "As part of the model, many teachers become teacher experts in particular strategies and act as mentors to others within their school who want to learn the strategy" (p. 68).

Expert Videos

In Chapter 4, we considered the use of videos as a vehicle for teachers examining their own instructional practices. Here we discuss the use of video clips as a way of demonstrating expert use of classroom strategies and behaviors. That is, for each of the 41 elements in Domain 1, a district should provide video clips of expert performance. Of course many of these clips would come from the ranks of the expert coaches in the district. The purpose of video clips is to allow teachers to observe what Ambady and Rosenthal (1992, 1993) refer to as "thin slices" of behavior that characterize expertise. These authors explain that expert behavior is often determined by and recognizable within relatively short episodes. To illustrate, consider again the strategy of withitness, which deals with adherence and lack of adherence to rules and procedures (Design Question 7) and typically occurs in lesson segments enacted on the spot. As we have seen, the general behaviors associated with this strategy include these:

- Physically occupying all quadrants of the room
- Scanning the entire room and making eye contact with all students
- Recognizing potential sources of disruption and dealing with them immediately
- Proactively addressing inflammatory situations

Certainly if a teacher simply performs these actions, it will increase his or her withitness. However, expert status regarding these actions is a function of thin slices of behavior such as the facial expressions the teacher uses while scanning the room or the manner in which the teacher employs body position and physical proximity while occupying all quadrants of the room.

Expert videos would capture these minute but important behaviors that change an effective strategy into a highly effective strategy. Over time, a district could acquire multiple examples of expert use of the strategies and behaviors from Domain 1. This library of videos would be a resource available to all teachers in a district. Some such video libraries already exist. For example, within the iObservation system (Learning Sciences International, 2009), a video library of multiple examples of each of the 41 elements of Domain 1 provides expert commentary on the thin slices of behavior associated with each strategy.

Teacher-Led Professional Development

It is probably safe to say that the most common model of professional development in K–12 education is to bring in a "consultant" during professional development days. That consultant commonly addresses the entire faculty in a school, or even an entire district, imparting information on some topic presumably of interest to all members of the faculty. Although this practice has a use in some situations, we propose that the norm in professional development should be teachers within the district or school conducting workshops and seminars. Again, these teachers would be drawn from the ranks of the expert coaches in a district. During professional development days, these teachers would hold workshops on the instructional skills for which they have been recognized. The other teachers in the district would attend those workshops that are most closely related to their professional growth and development plans. For example, during a given professional development day, workshops might be offered for each of the following topics:

- Withitness strategies
- Previewing strategies
- Summarizing and note-taking strategies
- Strategies for tracking student progress
- Strategies for communicating high expectations for all students

Teachers in the district would select from this menu of offerings those professional development experiences that most closely meet their needs and interests.

Another way for teachers to share ideas is through gallery walks. The term *gallery walk* is derived from the practice of patrons of the arts walking through a gallery. Each piece of art represents expert performance focused on a different topic and employing different technical strategies. The same process has been used with teachers. For example, as part of a monthly faculty meeting, volunteer teachers might exhibit artifacts from their students generated by specific strategies they have used in their classes. The gallery walk might be housed in the library with teacher displays at tables positioned around the library. As teachers walk around the room stopping at different display tables, the artifacts would be explained by those teachers hosting the display.

A variation of the gallery walk is the teacher science fair. Reeves (2008) describes the teacher science fair in the following way: "A growing number of schools throughout the United States use this approach. The most common model is a simple three-panel display board with student achievement results in the left-hand panel, teacher and leadership actions in the middle panel, and the conclusions and inferences from the data in the right-hand panel" (p. 72). As with the gallery walk, teachers peruse the three-panel displays and ask questions of the teachers who created the displays.

Virtual Communities

The establishment of professional learning communities (PLCs) in recent years has become a dominant educational reform strategy. According to Rick DuFour and his colleagues (DuFour, DuFour, & Eaker, 2008; DuFour & Eaker, 1998; DuFour, Eaker, & DuFour, 2005), the essence of a professional learning community is a collaborative culture that seeks to achieve measurable improvement goals through inquiry, deliberate actions, and a commitment to continuous improvement. DuFour and colleagues also note that school and district leaders must provide the means and structures for teachers to collaborate if professional learning communities are to be successful.

The challenge of how to organize teachers and also find time for collaboration is a constant struggle for schools. With the recent explosion of Web technologies, schools have slowly begun to move from professional learning communities located within the schools to global virtual communities encompassing diverse groups of teachers. Virtual communities are growing in use because they provide teachers with flexible access to each other at any time, from any place. Charalambos, Michalinos, and Chamberlain (2004) and Kleinman (2001) have suggested that virtual communities of practice can be an important element in enabling, establishing, and spreading professional norms of practice.

Virtual communities of practice typically use asynchronous communication tools often referred to as discussion forums or discussion threads. Using these tools, teachers do not have to be present at the same time to participate. Subsequently, teachers within a group can post ideas, messages, and questions so that all participants within the group can read these messages. This allows conversations to evolve and communities to develop over a period of time. Synchronous forms of communication involve participants in communication at the same time such as in a telephone conversation, instant messaging, or a chat. According to Jaffe, Moir, Swanson, and Wheeler (2006), asynchronous discourse is inherently self-reflective and, therefore, more conducive to deep learning than is synchronous discourse.

Technology can create powerful opportunities to organize teachers within schools, across the district or state, or nationally or globally to supplement and expand face-to-face professional learning communities. One example of work in this area is being conducted by Learning Sciences International (LSI), which has developed a wide array of virtual tools through a system call iObservation. Within the LSI system, teachers can engage in private, virtual conferences with a peer or supervisor or participate in discussions with fellow teachers, coaches, or administrators in vertical and/or horizontal grade-level configurations within the school or across the district. As illustrated in Figure 5.1, virtual conferencing provides a reciprocal means for teachers, coaches, and administrators to provide feedback to each other regarding their observations and insights about teaching and learning.

The discussion feature within a virtual community provides a place where groups of teachers can communicate, collaborate, reflect, and refine their practices by having group discussions, uploading lesson plans, and reviewing student work or other artifacts of classroom instruction.

Summary

This chapter addressed providing opportunities for teachers to observe and discuss expertise. Without such opportunities, teachers are left with trial and

FIGURE 5.1	Virtual Conferencing

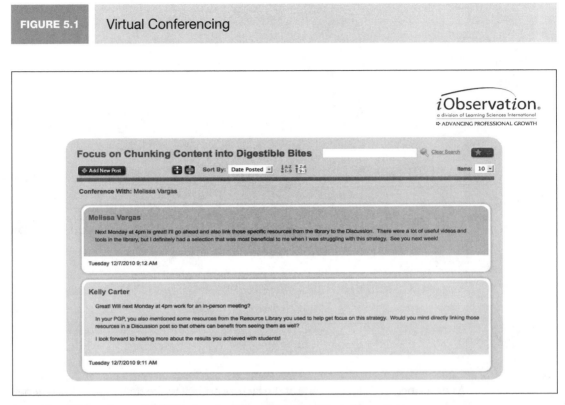

Source: From "iObservation.com," ©2010 by Learning Sciences International. Used with permission.

error as the primary technique for developing expertise. Five techniques were presented. Instructional rounds allow teachers to observe and learn from other teachers. Expert coaches should be drawn from the ranks of experienced teachers in the district who have established their effectiveness at enhancing student achievement. These coaches serve as resources to all teachers in a district. Expert videos are clips of teachers demonstrating effective practice in the strategies and behaviors from Domain 1. Over time, a district can and should develop an extensive library of clips to serve as a resource for teachers seeking examples of expert performance. Teacher-led professional development can manifest as gallery walks, teacher science fairs, and teachers providing workshops focused on specific strategies and behaviors. Finally, virtual communities can be used to enhance teacher discussions about expertise in an asynchronous manner. This technique allows for professional dialogue among teachers at a variety of times and in a variety of places.

CHAPTER 6

Clear Criteria and a Plan for Success

As described in Chapter 1, one of the factors critical to the development of teacher expertise is clear criteria for success. Without clear criteria for success, it is difficult to determine if one is progressing in one's skill development. Outside education, criteria for success tend to be explicit. To illustrate, a chess player would have little way of determining if her study of various chess moves was increasing her acumen unless she engaged in chess matches. A golfer would have little way to determine if practicing with different clubs for different purposes was actually paying off unless he played rounds of golf. Along with criteria for success, plans are necessary to achieve expertise. Plans include goals and resources needed to accomplish those goals. The chess player seeking to improve her level of expertise sets specific goals regarding techniques on which to improve and matches to win, as does the golfer. Teachers seeking expert status should follow suit.

In this chapter, we address the related issues of clear criteria for success and effective plans. We begin with criteria for success. Regarding effective teaching, two major categories of criteria should be used to determine success: (1) classroom strategies and behaviors and (2) value-added student achievement in the classroom. In her review of the research on metrics for measuring teacher effectiveness, David (2010) makes the case that use of both of these categories of criteria is superior to using either category in isolation.

Criteria for Classroom Strategies and Behaviors

Domain 1 addresses classroom strategies and behaviors. As depicted in Figure 1.2 in Chapter 1, it has the most direct link to student achievement. As we have seen in Chapter 4, teachers can receive feedback regarding their use of specific strategies and behaviors in a variety of ways, including teacher self-rating, walk-throughs, comprehensive observations, cueing teaching, and student surveys.

Using these multiple sources of data, a teacher can identify a small set of classroom strategies and behaviors on which to work over a year. We commonly recommend that teachers select at least one strategy or behavior from each of the three major types of lesson segments in Domain 1: routine segments, content segments, and segments that must be enacted on the spot. Within our model, teacher selection of specific Domain 1 elements on which to improve is critical. It not only provides focus for teachers but also puts them at the center of the development process. Commenting on this approach, Semadeni (2010) notes, "Imagine a school that allows each teacher to choose the area of teaching he or she most wants to grow in, provides time during contract hours to study best practices in that area, and then rewards that teacher for improving his or her teaching skills" (p. 66).

While teacher self-determination is important to our approach, the selection of strategies and behaviors on which a teacher will work over a year can be a negotiated decision. That is, using data from a variety of sources, a teacher and supervisor can jointly determine the specific strategies on which to work.

Tracking Progress

Once strategies and behaviors on which to focus have been identified, a teacher can systematically track his or her progress. This was depicted in Figure 4.8, but for ease of discussion, we provide a similar depiction in Figure 6.1. Figure 6.1 depicts five scores for a specific teacher over a three-month period. As mentioned in Chapter 4, these scores can come from a variety of sources. In fact, each of the scores recorded in Figure 6.1 can be a summary or composite score across two or more scores from different sources. For example, the second score might be a composite of the teacher's self-rating and a score provided by administrators from a walkthrough. To validate composite scores, teachers might be asked to keep all data about their performance in a file or portfolio so they can explain how composite scores were derived. For example, if asked, the teacher could explain that the second score was a composite of his self-rating of 2 and the rating of 1 provided from a comprehensive observation. The teacher would explain that after the postconference and ensuing discussion, the observer agreed that the teacher was very close to a score of 2 if a few minor corrections were made.

Upon making those corrections, the composite score for the strategy at that point was determined to be a 2.

Criteria for Student Achievement

We have referred throughout this book to the fact that student achievement is the superordinate goal regarding teacher expertise. Stated differently, advancements in Domains 1 through 4 are the means to enhanced student achievement. This is very much in keeping with the focus of the No Child Left Behind Act (NCLB) enacted in 2001 (see Marzano & Waters, 2009). It is also in keeping with the focus of the subsequent administrations (Editorial Projects in Education, 2009). It is probably safe to say that student achievement will be the focus of school reform for decades to come even as NCLB is altered or replaced.

One thing that is changing since the inception of NCLB is the metric used to gauge student achievement. The initial emphasis was on student "status," which

| FIGURE 6.1 | Five Ratings Recorded Over Three Months for a Teacher |

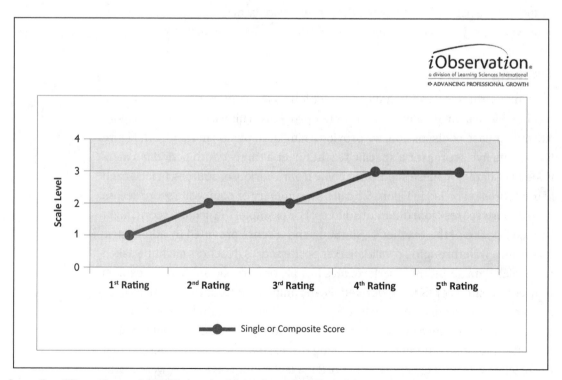

Source: From "iObservation.com," ©2010 by Learning Sciences International. Used with permission.

refers to students' scores at a particular point. Within the original design of NCLB, all students were expected to be at high levels of achievement. Indeed, schools and districts were to be judged on the extent to which they deviated from the criterion of no child being below established achievement standards. Marzano and Waters (2009) identified a number of pitfalls associated with this approach: many schools and districts have highly transient populations, schools and districts have great variability in the demographics of their students, and status-oriented assessments provide little useful information that can be used by schools and districts to improve their performance. For these reasons and others, many assessment experts have called for a value-added approach to measuring student achievement. As Barton (2006) noted:

> If we had an accountability system that truly measured student gain—sometimes called *growth* or *value added*—we could use whether students in any year have gained enough in that school year to show adequate progress. The end goal should not be achieving set scores by 2014. The goal should be reaching a standard for *how much* growth we expect during a school year in any particular subject. (p. 30)

Here we consider how a value-added approach can be employed with a primary emphasis on assessment data at the classroom level. The first step in constructing a value-added approach to measuring student achievement is to consider the types of assessments that will be used.

Types of Assessments

A variety of types of assessments might be used to measure value-added achievement. State assessments have high visibility but are administered only once per year, rendering them poor vehicles to be sensitive to learning over short intervals of time. Additionally, state assessments are administered in core subject areas only. Finally, state assessments might not reflect what is taught in class. Unless a district has aligned its local curriculum to the state assessments, there is no guarantee that state assessments actually measure what students have learned in a particular class.

A number of districts have developed end-of-course assessments. These are similar to state assessments in that they are given once a year only and are not good vehicles to address learning across short time intervals. However, they have the advantage of being closely tied to the content addressed in class where state assessments might not be. End-of-course assessments are typically designed to be a comprehensive treatment of the content addressed in a course. Additionally, end-of-course assessments can be designed for any subject area.

Benchmark assessments are another common form of assessment designed at the district level. One of the more useful aspects of benchmark assessments is that typically more than one assessment is available over the course of a given year, making them useful vehicles for picking up student learning during rather narrow intervals of time. Additionally, they are usually aligned with the content that has been addressed in class.

Common assessments focus on rather narrow topics and are even more numerous than benchmark assessments. Consequently, they can be used to measure student growth in achievement over relatively short intervals of time. Additionally, common assessments typically are tied directly to the curriculum taught in class.

Teacher-designed assessments are most closely related to what is taught in the classroom. In effect, the more classroom assessment data are used to determine student achievement, the closer the achievement data are to what actually occurs in the classroom. However, it must be kept in mind that teacher-designed assessments are the least reliable of all those mentioned thus far. This limitation does not mean that teacher-designed assessments should not be used to collect value-added achievement data. Indeed, they can and should be an integral part of the array of achievement data collected for an individual teacher.

Scales, as opposed to assessment, are growing in popularity, particularly as a way to measure value-added achievement. Marzano (2010b) has described the design and use of scales for this purpose. Briefly, scales have the generic form reported in Figure 6.2.

FIGURE 6.2	Generic Form of the Scale
Score 4.0	More complex content
Score 3.0	Target learning goal
Score 2.0	Simpler content
Score 1.0	With help, partial success at score 2.0 content and score 3.0 content
Score 0.0	Even with help, no success

© 2011 Robert J. Marzano

To understand the scale, it is best to start with score 3.0. To receive a score of 3.0, a student must demonstrate competence regarding the target learning goal. A score of 2.0 indicates competence regarding the simpler content, and a score of 4.0 indicates competence regarding the more complex content. Scores 4.0, 3.0, and 2.0 involve different content, then, while scores 1.0 and 0.0 do not. A score of

1.0 indicates that, independently, a student cannot demonstrate competence in the score 2.0 or 3.0 content, but, with help, he or she demonstrates partial competence. A score of 0.0 indicates that even with help, a student does not demonstrate competence or skill in any of the content.

Figure 6.3 uses a learning goal about heritable traits to illustrate a complete scale for a specific topic. Again, the score 3.0 content is the target learning goal. Thus, a teacher simply uses the target learning goal for the class as the score 3.0 content when designing a scale. The next whole-point score down is 2.0. The simpler content goes here. The next whole-point score up from the target learning goal (score 3.0) is 4.0. The more complex content goes there.

FIGURE 6.3	Scale for Heritable Traits
Score 4.0	Student will be able to discuss how heritable traits and nonheritable traits affect one another.
Score 3.0	Student will be able to differentiate heritable traits from nonheritable traits in real-world scenarios.
Score 2.0	Student will be able to recognize accurate statements about and isolated examples of heritable and nonheritable traits.
Score 1.0	With help, partial success at score 2.0 content and score 3.0 content.
Score 0.0	Even with help, no success.

© 2011 Robert J. Marzano

The score values of 1.0 and 0.0 do not represent new content, but they do represent different levels of competence. Score 1.0 indicates that the student does not demonstrate competence in any of the content when working independently. However, with help, the student has partial success at the score 2.0 and score 3.0 content. Score 0.0 indicates that even with help, the student has no success at the score 3.0 or 2.0 content.

When scales are used, progress over time can be readily tracked because scores on the scale have the same meaning regarding students' level of knowledge regardless of the type of assessment that is used. This not the case with the other types of assessments described thus far. (For a complete discussion, see Marzano, 2010b.)

The final type of data that can be used to measure value-added achievement is individual students' self-report of their learning. Although this might seem like a relatively weak type of data, there is evidence to the contrary. In a meta-analysis of the relationship of 138 variables to student achievement, student self-reports regarding their achievement had the highest correlation with achievement as measured by traditional assessments (Hattie, 2009).

If a district or school has access to all the forms of assessment described here, it can generate a number of indices for value-added achievement. Here we consider three such indices. We begin with knowledge gain.

Knowledge Gain

One of the most straightforward indices of value-added student achievement is knowledge gain. Tucker and Stronge (2005) have chronicled the use of gain scores in teacher evaluation systems in various parts of the country. A gain score is simply the difference between a student's score at the end of some interval of time and the beginning of some point in time. For example, a teacher might begin a unit of instruction by administering a pre-test and end the unit by administering a post-test. An individual student's gain score would be the difference between his post-test score and his pre-test score. The pre- and post-test can be either the same test or parallel tests (i.e., tests that measure the same topic at the same level of difficulty).

Not all of the assessments described previously can be used to compute knowledge gain. Because state assessments and end-of-course assessments are administered once a year only, they do not lend themselves to gain scores. Although benchmark assessments are administered more than once per year, they are typically not numerous enough to pick up knowledge gain across short intervals of time. Common assessments, if numerous enough, are useful vehicles for knowledge gain. They can be designed around fairly specific topics, which allows them to be used to assess learning within a specific unit of instruction. Scales can also be used to address fairly specific topics. Finally, teacher-designed assessments can readily be used to measure knowledge gain.

Residual Scores

Residual scores are a powerful metric for value-added achievement. A residual score is the difference between a student's predicted score and his or her observed score. One of the biggest advantages of residual scores is that they can make use of assessments that are given only once per year, like state assessments and end-of-course assessments.

To compute a residual score, some initial measure of student achievement is required along with a measure of student achievement at the end of an interval of time such as a unit of instruction, a quarter, a semester, or even an entire year. The premeasure of achievement does not have to be the same as the postmeasure. For example, a common assessment might be used as the premeasure and an end-of-course assessment as the postmeasure. Based on the statistical correlation between the two measures, a predicted score for each student is computed. The predicted score for each student represents the expected score for the student given his or her initial status. The residual score is the difference between the student's actual or observed score at the end of some interval of time and the student's expected score. A positive residual score indicates the student is doing better than expected. A negative residual score indicates that the student is doing worse than expected. Consequently, a residual score might be interpreted as a tacit measure of the effects of classroom instruction. If students' residual scores are positive, a reasonable inference might be that instruction was exceptional. If students' residual scores are negative, a reasonable assumption is that classroom instruction was not very effective.

To illustrate the use of residual scores, consider Figure 6.4. Figure 6.4 depicts nine residual scores each for a different student within a particular teacher's class. Those residual scores above the horizontal line indicate that students have scored above their predicted scores. Those residual scores below the horizontal line indicate that students have scored below their predicted scores. In this case, seven students have scored above their predicted scores, and two students have scored below their predicted scores.

FIGURE 6.4	Residual Scores

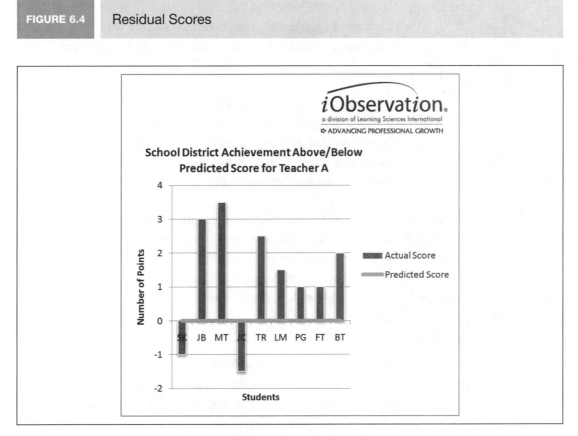

Source: From "iObservation.com," ©2010 by Learning Sciences International. Used with permission.

Student Self-Report of Knowledge Gain

The final value-added index that a district might use is student self-report of how much they learned. This can be acquired simply by administering Likert-type items like the following:

How much have you learned in this class?

0	1	2	3	4
Nothing				A Great Deal

The advantage to student self-report of knowledge gain is that it is quite easy to obtain. Likert items like the one here can be administered at the end of a unit of instruction or at the end of a quarter or a semester.

The Pitfalls of Value-Added Indices

Regardless of the value-added index that is used and the assessments used to generate these indices, it is important to remember that they are all imprecise attempts to measure the effects of teaching on student achievement. David (2010) cites a number of studies indicating conditions under which value-added measures can produce misleading information about teacher performance. She explains:

> Making judgments about individual teachers requires sophisticated analyses to sort out how much growth is probably caused by the teacher and how much is caused by other factors. For example, students who are frequently absent tend to have lower scores regardless of the quality of their teacher, so it is vital to take into account how many days students are present. (p. 81)

Ultimately, David concludes that multiple measures must be used to formulate opinions about teacher effectiveness: "To protect teachers from erroneous and harmful judgments, a consensus is emerging that we need multiple measures that tap evidence of good teaching practices as well as a variety of student outcomes, including but not limited to standardized test score gains" (p. 82).

Displaying Data

With value-added data available, a district can identify patterns of typical performance. For example, over time, a district can develop distributions of gain scores, residual scores, and student self-report scores. To illustrate, at Marzano Research Laboratory, over 493 average gain scores have been compiled for classes in which teachers employed pre-tests and post-tests using a 100-point scale. That distribution of gain scores is depicted in Figure 6.5.

In Figure 6.5, the median gain score (i.e., the 50th percentile) is 25.9. The 40th percentile average gain score is 22.6; the 60th percentile average gain score is 31.7, and so on. A distribution like this, using common assessments or benchmark assessments in a district, could be used to compare the average gain scores for individual teachers. The median gain score would be used as the measure of central tendency. Each year, each teacher's average gain score could be plotted in the district distribution as an indication of relative knowledge gain for students. A teacher with an average gain score of 38 points would be about 20 percentile

FIGURE 6.5	Distribution of Gain Scores Across 493 Classes

Percentile	Average Gain Score
1	0.0
5	1.2
10	4.9
15	8.8
20	11.7
25	15.4
30	17.8
35	20.0
40	22.6
45	24.2
50	25.9
55	28.5
60	31.7
65	34.9
70	37.7
75	41.1
80	43.8
85	48.4
90	56.7
95	68.2
99	89.6

points above the median. A teacher with an average gain score of 18 would be about 20 percentile points below the median. The same type of district distribution data could be compiled for residual scores and for students' self-reported knowledge gain.

Another way to display value-added data is to examine differences between ethnic groups or socioeconomic groups. For example, Figure 6.6 shows the average gain scores for students in one teacher's class who qualify for free and reduced lunch and students who do not qualify.

| FIGURE 6.6 | Average Gain Scores for Free and Reduced Lunch Students (FRL) Compared to Other Students (OTH) for Teacher A |

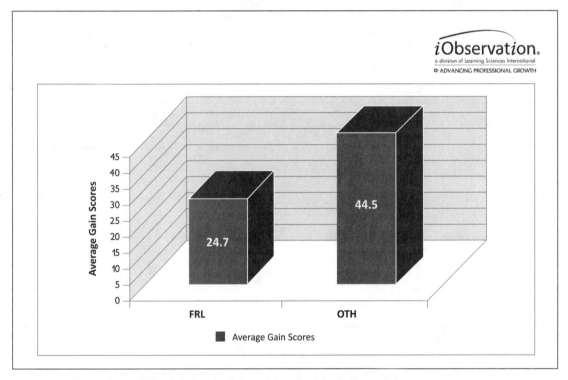

Source: From "iObservation.com," ©2010 by Learning Sciences International. Used with permission.

In this case, the gain score of students in the free and reduced lunch (FRL) category is lower than the gain score for students not in the free and reduced lunch (OTH) category. This comparison can be a powerful metric in determining the effectiveness of instruction for individual teachers. If the gain scores of students classified as eligible for free and reduced lunches are lower than those of other students, it might indicate differential or even inequitable effects of instruction in this particular class. The same comparisons can be made using residual scores and student self-report scores. Comparisons could also be made for different ethnic groups as opposed to socioeconomic status.

Professional Growth and Development Plans

With criteria in place for classroom strategies and behaviors (Domain 1) and for value-added student achievement, teachers can construct professional growth and development plans. Such plans are formal ways for teachers to set goals and articulate strategies to accomplish those goals. In his book *Successful Teacher Evaluation*, McGreal (1983) outlined the importance of goal setting and planning to teacher evaluation. He explained that teachers must be honored as professionals and as learners if the evaluation process is to help them develop their expertise. McGreal emphasized the utility of Bolton's (1973) goal-setting model as a tool in teacher evaluation. First, an area of need is identified. Next, a goal is established to address the need. Then, action is taken to address the need. After a period of time, the results are determined. If the results are satisfactory, the action continues as originally planned. If the results are not satisfactory, adjustments are made and the process is reengaged. We propose that professional development plans follow this same basic formula.

Formal professional development plans (PDPs) are required in many states. For example, the Wisconsin Department of Public Instruction (see Mahaffey, Lind, & Derse, 2005) describes PDPs in the following way:

It is up to the individual licensee to develop a PDP. The planning process for writing a PDP ensures that Wisconsin educators are broadly informed, deeply committed, and perform actions that will keep Wisconsin schools and districts places that motivate and engage all students and will result in enhanced student learning. The PDP is the property of the applicant.

The PDP serves as a mechanism for renewal of your license among you, a PDP Team, and the state superintendent. The plan must demonstrate your increased proficiency and professional development based on the Wisconsin Educator Standards . . .

This process allows you the opportunity to direct your own professional growth through a written PDP and indicate how that growth will affect student learning. (p. 2)

Primary and Secondary Goals

We propose that the goals within a professional growth and development plan should be thought of as two basic types: primary and secondary (see Figure 6.7). As shown in Figure 6.7, goals related to student achievement and classroom strategies and behaviors (Domain 1) are considered the primary goals within a professional growth and development plan. Domains 2, 3, and 4 articulate elements that are considered secondary or instrumental to the primary goals. A comprehensive professional growth and development plan, then, must focus on value-added achievement goals and Domain 1, but it must also include secondary goals that are drawn from Domains 2, 3, and 4. To illustrate, in a given year, a particular teacher might identify the following value-added achievement goals:

- The average gain score in my third period science class will be at the 60th percentile or above relative to the district norms.
- The average student self-reported knowledge gain score in that class will also be at the 60th percentile or higher.

Relative to Domain 1, the teacher might identify the following primary goals for the year:

Routine Segments

- I will increase my skill at having students track their progress on learning goals to the Applying Level (score 3) or higher.

Content Segments

- I will increase my skill at having students preview content to the Applying Level (score 3) or higher.

FIGURE 6.7 Primary and Secondary Goals

Focus	Goal Type
Student Value-Added Achievement	Primary
Domain 1: Classroom Strategies and Behaviors	Primary
Domain 2: Planning and Preparing	Secondary
Domain 3: Reflecting on Teaching	Secondary
Domain 4: Collegiality and Professionalism	Secondary

Segments Enacted on the Spot

- I will increase my skill at enhancing student engagement by using academic games to the Developing Level (score 2) or higher.

Note that a single goal in each of the three major categories of lesson segments has been identified by the teacher. We believe this to be a minimum expectation for every teacher each year. That is, each year every teacher is working on increasing his or her skill level in at least one strategy in every major category of lesson segments. Also note that the teacher has established specific goals for each of these three elements using the scales reported in Appendix A.

With specific primary goals identified, the teacher next will identify secondary goals that he or she perceives as instrumental in accomplishing the primary goals. It is important to emphasize that we are not recommending that every year each teacher tries to address all areas from Domains 2, 3, and 4. Just as specific areas of focus are selected from Domain 1 in a given year, so, too, are specific areas of focus selected from Domains 2, 3, and 4. Ideally, each year a teacher selects one or more elements from Domains 2, 3, and 4 that they believe are directly related to the successful completion of their primary goals relative to student achievement and Domain 1. We begin the discussion with Domain 2.

As described in Chapter 3, Domain 2, planning and preparing, has three categories of activities each with specific elements:

- Planning and preparing for lessons and units
  - Planning and preparing for effective scaffolding of information within lessons
  - Planning and preparing for lessons within a unit that progress toward a deep understanding and transfer of content
  - Planning and preparing for appropriate attention to established content standards

- Planning and preparing for use of materials and technology
  - Planning and preparing for the use of available materials for upcoming units and lessons (e.g., manipulatives, videotapes)
  - Planning and preparing for the use of available technologies, such as interactive whiteboards, reponse systems, and computers

- Planning and preparing for special needs of students
  - Planning and preparing for the needs of English language learners
  - Planning and preparing for the needs of special education students
  - Planning and preparing for the needs of students who come from home environments that offer little support for schooling

As is the case for the 41 elements in Domain 1, each element within Domain 2 has a specific scale that allows a teacher to identify his or her current level of performance and set a goal for future performance. These scales are found in Appendix D. Figure 6.8 reports the scale for the element "planning and preparing for effective scaffolding of information within lessons," which is in the general category of planning and preparing for lessons and units. This scale contains five values, just as the scales for the 41 elements in Domain 1. Again, the values are Not Using (0), Beginning (1), Developing (2), Applying (3), and Innovating (4). Not Using means the teacher makes no attempt to scaffold information. Beginning means that the teacher attempts to scaffold information but does not actually complete or follow through with these attempts. Developing means that the teacher scaffolds information but the relationship between elements is not clear. Applying means that the teacher organizes content in such a way that each piece of information clearly builds on the previous piece. Finally, Innovating means that the teacher is a recognized leader in helping others scaffold information in their lessons. In a given year, a teacher might establish a secondary goal to increase his or her competence in planning for effective scaffolding within lessons to a score of Applying or above.

FIGURE 6.8 Scale for Planning and Preparing for Effective Scaffolding of Information Within Lessons

Innovating (4)	Applying (3)	Developing (2)	Beginning (1)	Not Using (0)
The teacher is a recognized leader in helping others with this activity.	Within lessons, the teacher organizes content in such a way that each new piece of information clearly builds on the previous piece.	The teacher scaffolds the information, but the relationship among elements is not made clear.	The teacher attempts to perform this activity but does not actually complete or follow through with these attempts.	The teacher makes no attempt to perform this activity.

Domain 3 addresses reflecting on teaching. Again, each element within each category has an associated scale reported in Appendix E. In a given year, a teacher might set a secondary goal to increase his or her competence in this element to a score of Developing or above. Domain 4 addresses collegiality and professionalism. The scales for this domain are found in Appendix F. In a given year, a teacher might set a goal to enhance his or her skill at this activity to a score of Developing or above.

Within our model, each year each teacher would develop and implement a professional growth and development plan. Professional growth and development plans would be written and used as a formal part of a teacher's yearly evaluation.

As described earlier, the process of developing a professional growth and development plan involves identifying specific primary goals (goals for value-added achievement and Domain 1) and accompanying secondary or instrumental goals for Domain 2 (planning and preparing), Domain 3 (reflecting on teaching), and Domain 4 (collegiality and professionalism). As reported by McGreal (1983), Iwanicki (1981) explains that these plans should be evaluated at a number of stages. The first consideration is the quality of the plan itself. A second consideration is the extent to which the teacher uses the plan throughout the school year. The plan should be the blueprint for the teacher's activities regarding personal growth and development throughout the year. The final consideration is the extent to which the goals identified in the plan were actually attained. This would entail a summative evaluation conference at the end of a year with each teacher.

Summary

This chapter addressed clear criteria for success and a plan for success. Criteria for success should be established in two areas. The first is Domain 1, classroom strategies and behaviors. Each year, teachers should select specific strategies and behaviors from Domain 1 on which to improve and use the scales in Appendix A to track their development. The second area for which criteria should be established is student value-added achievement. Three general indices for value-added achievement were discussed: gain scores, residual scores, and student self-report of knowledge gain. With criteria established for Domain 1 and value-added achievement, teachers can develop professional growth and development plans. Two types of goals should be articulated in professional growth and development plans. Primary goals should be set for student value-added achievement and Domain 1. Secondary goals should be set for Domains 2, 3, and 4. Secondary goals are considered instrumental in accomplishing primary goals.

CHAPTER 7

Recognizing Expertise

Recognizing teacher expertise is the last element that a district or school must address if it is to provide a systemic approach to teacher development. Of course, any discussion of teacher recognition must encompass the topic of teacher evaluation.

Teacher Evaluation in the United States

Teacher evaluation has received a great deal of criticism in terms of its rigor and viability over the last few years. To illustrate, consider the following quote from the March 6, 2010, edition of *Newsweek*:

> At the same time, the teachers' unions have become more and more powerful. In most states, after two or three years, teachers are given lifetime tenure. It is almost impossible to fire them. In New York City in 2008, three out of 30,000 tenured teachers were dismissed for cause. The statistics are just as eye-popping in other cities. The percentage of teachers dismissed for poor performance in Chicago between 2005 and 2008 (the most recent figures available) was 0.1 percent. In Akron, Ohio, zero percent. In Toledo, 0.01 percent. In

Denver, zero percent. In no other socially significant profession are the workers so insulated from accountability. The responsibility does not just fall on the unions. Many principals don't even try to weed out the poor performers (or they transfer them to other schools in what's been dubbed the "dance of the lemons"). Year after year, about 99 percent of all teachers in the United States are rated "satisfactory" by their school systems; firing a teacher invites a costly court battle with the local union. (www.newsweek.com/id/234590)

Similar criticisms of teacher evaluation systems have been leveled by a number of popular reports. One of those reports is entitled *Rush to Judgment* (Toch & Rothman, 2008). It was discussed briefly in Chapter 2. As reported by Toch and Rothman, a study of the Chicago school system found that 87 percent of 600 schools did not issue a single "unsatisfactory" teacher rating between 2003 and 2006, even though 69 of those schools had been classified as failing educationally. Perhaps more striking is the fact that of all the teacher evaluations during those years, only 0.3 percent were "unsatisfactory." In contrast, 93 percent of the city's 25,000 teachers received "excellent" or "superior" ratings.

Additionally, the report paints a picture of the K–12 education system in this country that is almost devoid of substantive feedback to teachers. As reported by Toch and Rothman (2008), a study of the evaluation policies of the 50 largest U.S. systems produced the results in Figure 7.1 for untenured teachers:

FIGURE 7.1	Frequency of Evaluations for Tenured and Untenured Teachers in the 50 Largest Districts

Untenured Teachers	
Twice per year	20%
Once per year	52%
Once every two years	2%
Undetermined	26%
Tenured Teachers	
Once per year	34%
Once every two years	12%
Once every three years	14%
Once every five years	12%
Undetermined	28%

The findings reported in Figure 7.1 are striking, particularly when contrasted with the research on expertise. As described previously, to become an expert an individual must engage in focused practice and receive focused feedback for at least 10 years. The results reported in Figure 7.1 indicate that the largest 50 districts in the United States are not designed to provide either. Consider untenured teachers who require the most feedback. No district of the largest 50 provided feedback to untenured teachers more than twice per year, and only 20 percent provided feedback twice per year. For tenured teachers, no district provided feedback more than once per year, and only 34 percent provided feedback even once per year. Given that it requires at least 10 years to become an expert, districts would have to dramatically increase the amount of feedback to classroom teachers if they wish to enhance their pedagogical expertise.

Toch and Rothman (2008) further explain that static indicators like teacher credentials are not good predictors of whether students learn in a particular teacher's classroom:

> But recent studies have found that such qualifications [teacher licensure] don't guarantee effective teachers. A 2005 report on 9,400 Los Angeles teachers by Thomas Kane of Harvard and Douglas Staiger of Dartmouth, for example, found no meaningful differences in the achievement results of students taught by teachers who were certified and those taught by teachers who lacked certification. In some instances, the unlicensed teachers produced substantially higher results than their certified counterparts. (p. 2)

Another report entitled *The Widget Effect* (Weisberg et al., 2009), also mentioned in Chapter 2, provided similar conclusions about teacher evaluation. As explained in Chapter 2, the "widget effect" derives its unusual name from the assumption that the K–12 education system tends to treat teachers as "widgets"—parts of a system that are interchangeable and inconsequential to student achievement. The authors examined the practices of 12 districts across the country, along with existing state and district policies. Their overarching conclusion can be summed up in the following way: "Teacher effectiveness—the most important factor for schools in improving student achievement—is not measured, recorded, or used to inform decision-making in any meaningful way" (p. 3). To support this claim, they provide some compelling illustrations from the 12 districts they studied.

One distinction in the way feedback is provided to teachers is whether a district uses a binary scale to evaluate teachers (i.e., evaluate teachers as either Satisfactory or Unsatisfactory) as opposed to a scale with multiple categories (e.g., Outstanding, Very Good, Satisfactory, Improvement Needed, Unsatisfactory).

The authors of *The Widget Effect* are particularly critical of systems that employ a binary approach: "in districts that use binary ratings, virtually all tenured teachers (more than 99 percent) receive the satisfactory rating; the number receiving an unsatisfactory rating amounts to a fraction of a percentage. In these districts, it makes little difference that two ratings are available; in practice only one is ever used" (p. 11).

Even when multiple categories of evaluation are used, the results are similar. To illustrate, consider Figure 7.2, which lists the percentages of tenured teachers in each category of two multicategory systems employed by two urban districts in two midwestern states.

FIGURE 7.2	Distribution of Teachers Across a Multiple-Category Evaluation System in Two Urban Districts

District 1: 34,889 Tenured Teachers		
Rating	**Percent**	**Cumulative Percent**
Superior	68.75%	68.75%
Excellent	24.96%	93.65%
Satisfactory	6.1%	99.75%
Unsatisfactory	0.4%	100.15%
District 2: 1,062 Tenured Teachers		
Rating	**Percent**	**Cumulative Percent**
Outstanding	60.1%	60.1%
Very good	31.3%	91.4%
Satisfactory	8.0%	99.4%
Improvement needed	0.7%	100.1%
Unsatisfactory	0.0%	100.1%

Note: Cumulative percentages add up to over 100 due to rounding.

In the first district (with 34,889 tenured teachers), 68.75 percent had the highest rating. In the second district (with 1,062 tenured teachers), 60.1 percent had the highest rating. What is particularly disturbing is the percentage of teachers who received the lowest ratings and the highest ratings. In the first district, 0.4 percent received the lowest rating, yet 68.75 percent received the highest rating. In the second district, no tenured teachers received the lowest ratings, and 60 percent received the highest ratings. This makes little if any sense from a pure statistical perspective. To illustrate, Ericsson and Charness (1994) state that typically, only 2 percent of the individuals within any complex domain like teaching have reached the level of expert at any point in time. If the top categories of rating in the two districts reported in Figure 7.2 are intended to signal expert status, or even approaching expert status, then these districts and others like them with similar distributions of teacher ratings would be expected to exhibit exceptional achievement. Because the vast majority of teachers in their districts are at the high end of the distribution in terms of their pedagogical skills, the vast majority of their students would be expected to exhibit exceptional achievement. Unfortunately, this is not the case. Districts that have a majority of highly rated teachers many times have student achievement levels that are quite low (see Toch & Rothman, 2008; Weisberg et al., 2009). Clearly, the evaluation system in many, if not most, districts is lacking. This is evident to teachers themselves. Witness the following comments reported by Weisberg and colleagues when teachers in their study districts were surveyed:

> "Poorly performing teachers are rated at the same level as the rest of us. This infuriates those of us who do a good job." (Teacher) (p. 10)

> "New teachers are given so little support in my district that sometimes they are simply doomed to fail. Yet, no one notices and they finish their probationary status without a negative evaluation." (Teacher) (p. 15)

> "I think it gives hard working, honest teachers a bad reputation being lumped together with a group of sub-par teachers. What's even worse is that our principal does absolutely nothing about any of this." (Teacher) (p. 16)

> "It is the easiest thing for administrators to do. It's the path of least resistance. They don't have time or often, even the authority, to coach or correct ineffective teachers. The good teachers remain unrewarded for doing fantastic jobs, while bad teachers get to coast along." (Teacher) (p. 19)

> "I do not feel adequately trained to conduct a teacher evaluation. There are evaluation tools, but no one reviews them with you. We are not trained on the process. As a first year principal, you try it and you move through the process because it has to be done." (Principal, p. 21)

> "Many teachers are accustomed to receiving a 'superior' rating and simply do not accept anything lower. It also seems to be an easier way out for administrators, rather than have a confrontation with a teacher." (Teacher, p. 22)

"There are teachers who pour their heart and souls into teaching. It is heartbreaking to know that all students may have gained in your classroom will not be continued as they move forward. This causes resentment and frustration in our school culture." (Teacher, p. 24)

"The evaluation process should have teacher development as the primary goal, not just assigning a number on a rubric. As it is set up now, there is no immediate feedback to the teacher in any constructive format. Scores are based on rigid, often meaningless recitations. It is the epitome of poor teaching methods to give a score without discussion." (Teacher, p. 14)

Finally, even teacher unions, commonly credited with blocking reforms in teacher evaluation, seem to recognize the benefits of a more rigorous and fair system. Again quoting from a statement provided by the Pueblo Education Association whose district was part of the Weisberg et al. (2009) study:

"I believe that all stakeholders should come together to create a more credible, meaningful, and productive system for teacher, administrator, and school effectiveness evaluations. Teachers are professionals who value their chosen career and would like to work with colleagues who are excited and knowledgeable about their fields and teaching in general. Teachers and administrators working together in a system which promotes teachers as professionals and supports their professional development to meet the needs of their students, increase instructional quality, and develop effective curriculum is a benefit to all." Pueblo Education Association (CO) (p. 40)

Progress in Teacher Evaluation

Teacher evaluation in this country can be characterized as a monolith with substantial inertia regarding the evaluation process. This inertia is a result of little, if any, serious attempt to alter teacher evaluation practices. Consequently, one might reasonably predict that teacher evaluation is not likely to change radically in the near future. This fact notwithstanding, the first decade of the 21st century has provided evidence for a loosening of the inertia holding teacher evaluation in a static state.

In 2000, the Teacher Advancement Program (TAP) was started by businessman Lowell Milken. The TAP model received considerable attention as a performance for pay program. However, that component represents just one facet of the approach. The program allows schools to identify a common set of characteristics of good teaching and then use peer mentors and master teachers to work with colleagues to improve the skills of teachers (Sawchuk, 2009). The program is based on four major components. The first component allows teachers to ascend a career ladder where they move from a career teacher; to a mentor teacher who leads in professional development efforts; to a master who team teaches, does demonstration lessons, and observes other teachers. The second component is ongoing professional development and coaching whereby master teachers lead collaborative teams that focus on student work and effective teaching practices. The third component is a system of instructionally focused accountability measures whereby teachers receive developmental and summative feedback based on a series of rubrics that describe their teaching in a variety of areas. The final component is a performance-based compensation model that allows teachers to earn extra pay based on a combination of the achievement of students in their classroom, schoolwide achievement, and teaching evaluations. Many of the elements of the TAP model mirror the recommendations in this book.

Another indicator of the changing landscape regarding teacher evaluation is the apparent success of the National Board of Professional Teaching Standards (NBPTS). As described in Chapter 1, NBPTS had its genesis in the latter part of the 20th century from the deliberations of Albert Shanker and the Carnegie Corporation of New York. Currently, it is estimated that some 82,000 teachers have achieved NBPTS certification in spite of the fact that teachers must pay to begin and complete the process. Additionally, the process is complex and time-consuming.

The NBPTS certification process is based on five underlying assumptions or propositions that "summarize the knowledge, skills, dispositions, and beliefs" that would characterize an NBPTS-endorsed teacher (www.nbpts.org):

1. Teachers evidence commitment to students and their learning by, among other things, "making knowledge accessible to all students," by "treating students equitably," and by having in-depth knowledge of how students develop and learn.

2. Teachers demonstrate "mastery over the subject(s) they teach" as well as competence in the instructional strategies that are most applicable to that subject.

3. Teachers are "responsible for managing and monitoring student learning," including keeping students "motivated, engaged and focused." This third proposition also speaks to competence in both individual and group assessment of student learning.

4. Teachers systematically and critically reflect on their practice as the foundation for continuous improvement.

5. Teachers "collaborate with others to improve student learning."

It is the responsibility of a teacher seeking NBPTS certification to submit a portfolio of classroom practice that includes written descriptions of teaching episodes, accompanying student work, video recordings of interactions with students, and evidence of accomplishments outside the classroom that have an impact on student learning. A $500 nonrefundable fee is required to initiate the portfolio construction process. After the portfolio is completed and submitted, each NBPTS candidate takes an online assessment of content-area knowledge in six constructed-response exercises. Final certification is based on the successful evaluation of both the portfolio and the online assessment, and the payment of an additional $2,000 fee. Once certified, the NBPTS certification is good for 10 years (Sawchuk, 2010). Again, many of the NBPTS processes mirror the recommendations in this book.

A New Perspective on Teacher Evaluation

At the beginning of this book, we noted that the basic purpose of teacher supervision and evaluation is to enhance teacher effectiveness. In this chapter, we focus on the topic of evaluation where previous chapters have focused on supervision. By design, our treatment of the topic of teacher evaluation is brief and surface level in nature. We do not address topics like licensure, tenure, and merit pay, although these are important issues and, we believe, can be informed by some of the distinctions articulated in this text. For informative discussions of these topics, see Cochran-Smith and Power (2010), Grossman and Loeb (2010), and Johnson and Papay (2010).

Fundamentally, the previous chapters have laid out a system in which teachers consistently receive multiple forms of feedback that are used as the basis for growth in specific skills within specific domains of teacher competence. Teachers also receive multiple indicators of value-added student achievement such as gain scores and residual scores. As discussed in Chapter 6, these metrics considered in isolation can produce erroneous conclusions about teachers. However, considered in the aggregate, measures of teacher growth in pedagogy (Domain 1) and student value-added achievement can provide the foundation for a more rigorous and informative approach to teacher evaluation. As reported by David (2010), at least one study indicates that most teachers support a multiple-level approach (Coggshall, Ott, & Lasagna, 2010). Toch and Rothman (2008) articulate similar sentiments:

> Comprehensive evaluations—with standards and scoring rubrics and multiple classroom observations by multiple evaluators and a role for student work and teacher reflection—are valuable regardless of the degree to which they predict student achievement, and regardless of whether they're used to

weed out a few bad teachers or a lot of them. They contribute much more to the improvement of teaching than today's drive-by evaluations or test scores alone. And they contribute to a much more professional atmosphere in schools.

As a result, they make public school teaching more attractive to the sort of talent that the occupation has struggled to recruit and retain. Capable people want to work in environments where they sense they matter, and using evaluation systems as engines of professional improvement signals that teaching is such an enterprise. Comprehensive evaluation systems send a message that teachers are professionals doing important work. (p. 13)

Under the assumption that a district has multiple measures regarding teacher expertise in Domain 1 and value-added student achievement, we have one primary recommendation (for now) regarding the process of teacher evaluation: *Teacher evaluation should recognize different stages of development progressing toward expertise.*

As described previously in this chapter, some districts use yearly evaluation systems that employ multiple categories of teacher performance such as Superior, Excellent, Satisfactory, and Unsatisfactory. This is not the same as recognizing different stages of teaching expertise, at least as we define it. Stages of teaching expertise are not assigned on a year-to-year basis. Rather, they represent stages that a teacher progresses through on the path to expert status. In fact, we believe attempts to assign yearly scores to teachers regarding their performance particularly as it relates to value-added achievement will always be flawed simply because of the imprecision of value-added achievement scores and scores that reflect performance in Domain 1. However, it is possible to observe and document progress over time through clearly defined stages of expertise. Figure 7.3 depicts a possible sequence of stages.

The first stage in Figure 7.3 is referred to as the Initial Status Teacher. The criteria for membership in this category are value-added achievement scores below the 34th percentile on district norms. Stated differently, the value-added achievement of these teachers is in the bottom one-third of scores across the entire district. Although such scores are relatively low, they are typical for beginning teachers, who would not be expected to produce student value-added achievement that is equal to or superior to more experienced teachers. Relative to Domain 1, teachers in this category are working to obtain minimum scores of Beginning (1) on all Domain 1 strategies and behaviors. To move to the next category, one criterion is that these teachers must demonstrate that they can accurately execute strategies and behaviors in all elements of Domain 1 even though they might not be particularly fluent with these strategies and behaviors. Stated differently,

FIGURE 7.3	Stages of Teacher Development

Stage	Achievement and Domain 1 Criteria	Responsibilities
Initial Status Teacher	• Value-added achievement scores below the 34 percentile on district norms • Minimum scores of Beginning (1) on all elements of Domain 1	• Continue to work on improving student value-added achievement scores by increasing expertise in selected Domain 1 strategies and behaviors. • Interact with other teachers about effective practice in Domain 1 and Domain 2 (Planning and Preparing). • Work in Domains 3 and 4.
Professional Teacher	• Value-added achievement scores between the 34th and 84th percentile on district norms • Minimum scores of Developing (2) and a majority of scores of Applying (3) for Domain 1 • Minimum scores of Developing (2) in Domains 2, 3, and 4	• Continue to work on improving value-added achievement scores and increasing expertise in selected Domain 1 strategies and behaviors. • Interact with other teachers about effective practices in Domain 1. • Lead interactions about Domain 2. • Continue working in Domains 3 and 4.
Mentor Teacher	• Value-added achievement scores between 85th and 97th percentile on district norms • Scores of Innovating (4) on selected elements of Domain 1 that represent the teacher's personal formula for effective teaching and minimum scores of 3 on all other elements • Minimum scores of 2 in Domains 2, 3, and 4 and a majority of scores of 3 or above	• Work with Initial Status Teachers and Professional Teachers to enhance their skills in Domains 1 and 2. • Function as an expert coach. • Lead instructional rounds. • Continue working in Domain 3. • Take a leadership role in Domain 4.
Master Teacher	• Value-added achievement scores above the 97th percentile on district norms • Scores of Innovating (4) on selected elements of Domain 1 that represent the teacher's personal formula for effective teaching and minimum scores of 3 on all other elements • Minimum scores of 3 on all elements of Domains 2, 3, and 4	• Work with Initial Stage Teachers and Professional Teachers to enhance their skills in Domains 1 and 2. • Lead instructional rounds. • Function as an expert coach. • Take a leadership role in Domain 4. • Work with district administrators to set policy for teacher evaluation, and engage in teacher evaluation.

to move beyond the Initial Status category, teachers must demonstrate a minimum score of 2 on all Domain 1 strategies and behaviors. The primary responsibility of Initial Status Teachers is to continue increasing their skills in Domain 1 strategies and behaviors. To do so, they are expected to interact with other teachers about

Domain 1 and Domain 2, seeking mentorship and help. They must also reflect on their own teaching (Domain 3) and engage in activities that promote collegiality and professionalism (Domain 4).

The second stage in Figure 7.3 is called the Professional Teacher. The criteria for membership in this category are value-added achievement scores between the 34th and 84th percentiles on district norms. Additionally, Professional Teachers have minimum scores of Developing (2) in all elements of Domain 1 and a majority of scores of Applying (3) or above. This is not to say that Professional Teachers systematically use strategies and behaviors in all 41 elements of Domain 1. In fact, Professional Teachers will most probably have identified strategies that they typically rely on in their classrooms. However, a Professional Teacher has demonstrated that he or she could execute all the strategies and behaviors in Domain 1 if called on to do so. In addition to these criteria, the Professional Teacher has attained minimum scores of Developing (2) on all elements of Domain 2, Domain 3, and Domain 4. The responsibilities of Professional Teachers are to continue to work on improving the value-added achievement scores of their students and to increase their expertise in selected Domain 1 strategies and behaviors. The Professional Teacher interacts with other teachers about Domain 1 strategies, as does the Initial Status Teacher. In addition, the Professional Teacher leads discussions regarding Domain 2, planning and preparing. The Professional Teacher still continues to develop expertise in Domains 3 and 4. Most probably, all teachers would be required to reach the status of Professional Teacher if they are to maintain employment in a district.

The third stage in Figure 7.3 is the Mentor Teacher. Teachers would not be required to reach this status to maintain employment in a district. That is, a teacher could maintain indefinite employment in a district without ever rising above the stage of Professional Teacher. Criteria for inclusion in the category of Mentor Teacher include value-added achievement scores between the 85th and 97th percentiles on district norms. Regarding Domain 1, the Mentor Teacher has no score below 3 and scores of 4 on selected elements of Domain 1. These areas of exceptional performance in Domain 1 constitute the signature style of Mentor Teachers. In addition to their skills in Domain 1, Mentor Teachers exhibit minimum scores of 2 on all elements of Domains 2, 3, and 4 and a majority of scores of 3 or above. The responsibilities of Mentor Teachers include working with Initial Status Teachers and Professional Teachers to enhance their skills in Domains 1 and 2. They also lead instructional rounds and function as expert coaches, as described in Chapter 5. While they continue to develop their own expertise in Domain 3, they take a leadership role in Domain 4, collegiality and professionalism.

The final stage in Figure 7.3 is the Master Teacher. Relatively few teachers in a district will reach this status. Criteria for inclusion in the Master Teacher category include value-added achievement scores above the 97th percentile on district norms. Regarding Domain 1, the Master Teacher has the same criteria as the Mentor Teacher—scores of 4 on selected elements of Domain 1 and minimum scores of 3 on all other elements. Relative to Domains 2, 3, and 4, the Master Teacher has minimum scores of 3 on all elements. In short, the Master Teacher has no score below 3 on any element of Domains 1, 2, 3, and 4. The responsibilities of the Master Teacher include working with Initial Status Teachers on Domain 1 and Domain 2. This is similar to the Mentor Teacher. Also like the Mentor Teacher, the Master Teacher leads instructional rounds, serves as an expert coach, and takes a leadership role in Domain 4. Unlike the Mentor Teacher, the Master Teacher works with district administrators to set policies regarding teacher evaluation. Additionally, the Master Teacher is intimately involved in the teacher evaluation process.

Where Does a District Begin?

The initiatives described in this chapter and the previous chapter are ambitious and, when fully implemented, represent a paradigm shift in teacher feedback and teacher evaluation. Indeed, when fully implemented, the suggestions in this book represent a paradigm shift in the entire culture of K–12 education. Marzano et al. (2005) have detailed the travails of paradigm shift within a district or school. Some of these include living with the perceptions by some that the district or school is not responsive to the needs of its constituents, and the perception that the district or school is moving backward as opposed to forward. Indeed, during paradigm shift, a district or school might lose some trusted educators for whom the change is simply too dramatic.

Given the complexities of paradigm shift, we do not recommend that a district or school attempt to implement our suggestions hastily. Rather, the changes recommended in this book can be implemented in an incremental fashion.

Perhaps the first step for a district is to adopt or adapt the elements we have outlined in Domain 1—classroom strategies and behaviors. We refer to this as developing a common "language of instruction." Districts and schools with which we have worked commonly spend about a year becoming familiar with the strategies and behaviors in Domain 1 by studying the book *The Art and Science of Teaching* (Marzano, 2007) or *A Handbook for the Art and Science of Teaching* (Marzano & Brown, 2009) or both. At the end of that year, they formally adopt or adapt the model as their official language of instruction—the official vocabulary, if you will, that teachers and administrators will use to interact about teaching.

During the second year, districts and schools put heavy emphasis on instructional rounds. This can be done initially on a voluntary basis. Recall from the discussion in Chapter 5 that the purpose of instructional rounds is for teachers to observe other teachers practicing their craft so that they might compare the classroom strategies and behaviors they observe with those they use in their own classrooms. The purpose of instructional rounds is not to evaluate teachers who are being observed. In fact, it is typically considered an honor to be asked to be observed during rounds because it implies that the teacher is recognized for skillfully employing instructional strategies and behaviors. During the second year, teachers might also be asked to score themselves on each of the 41 elements of Domain 1 using the scales in Appendix A. This self-rating might be kept confidential by the teacher during this year. That is, the purpose of the self-ratings during this year is for teachers to identify their own strengths and weaknesses in Domain 1. This awareness helps focus teachers' attention while they are engaged in instructional rounds. Since one purpose for the second year is to help teachers become more familiar with the elements of Domain 1 and to establish a culture of teachers sharing ideas and learning from one another, there might be little reason for teacher self-ratings to be disclosed to administrators or supervisors.

From the third year on, the district or school becomes more formal about the process of supervision and evaluation. Domains 2, 3, and 4 are introduced. Teachers begin formally writing professional growth and development plans and identify primary and secondary goals as described in Chapter 6. At some point, teachers' progress on primary and secondary goals become a formal part of the evaluation process, and the stages of professional development described earlier in this chapter (i.e., Initial Status Teacher, Professional Teacher, Mentor Teacher, and Master Teacher) are implemented.

Seizing the Moment

We believe that the face of teacher supervision and evaluation is changing rapidly in K–12 education in the United States. Hardly a week goes by without some story appearing in the news about a district or state changing its approach to supervision and evaluation. In this book, we have attempted to articulate a framework that can be used by districts to guide those changes. We encourage educators who read this book to make adaptations to our work. Indeed, no framework can meet the needs of every district.

Although we encourage districts and schools to adapt our work to meet their specific needs, we do not encourage districts to tarry when initiating the changes recommended in this book. Implementing substantive changes in a staged fashion is advisable, but waiting until all constituents within a district are completely comfortable with the changes is a recipe for inaction. In our opinion, now is the optimum time for bold moves in teacher supervision and evaluation. We hope that this book provides some concrete suggestions for those bold moves and, perhaps more important, helps motivate those administrators in a position of power and responsibility to initiate those moves immediately.

Observational Protocol (Long Form)

LESSON SEGMENTS INVOLVING ROUTINE EVENTS

Design Question 1: What will I do to establish and communicate learning goals, track student progress, and celebrate success?

1. Providing Clear Learning Goals and Scales to Measure Those Goals

The teacher provides a clearly stated learning goal accompanied by scale or rubric that describes levels of performance relative to the learning goal.	*Notes*

Teacher Evidence	**Student Evidence**
☐ Teacher has a learning goal posted so that all students can see it. ☐ The learning goal is a clear statement of knowledge or information as opposed to an activity or assignment. ☐ Teacher makes reference to the learning goal throughout the lesson. ☐ Teacher has a scale or rubric that relates to the learning goal posted so that all students can see it. ☐ Teacher makes reference to the scale or rubric throughout the lesson.	☐ When asked, students can explain the learning goal for the lesson. ☐ When asked, students can explain how their current activities relate to the learning goal. ☐ When asked, students can explain the meaning of the levels of performance articulated in the scale or rubric.

Scale

	Innovating (4)	Applying (3)	Developing (2)	Beginning (1)	Not Using (0)
Providing clear learning goals and scales to measure those goals	Adapts and creates new strategies for unique student needs and situations	Provides a clearly stated learning goal accompanied by a scale or rubric that describes levels of performance, and monitors students' understanding of the learning goal and the levels of performance	Provides a clearly stated learning goal accompanied by a scale or rubric that describes levels of performance	Uses strategy incorrectly or with parts missing	Strategy was called for but not exhibited

© 2011 Robert J. Marzano

2. Tracking Student Progress

The teacher facilitates tracking of student progress on one or more learning goals using a formative approach to assessment.

Notes

Teacher Evidence

☐ Teacher helps students track their individual progress on the learning goal.

☐ Teacher uses formal and informal means to assign scores to students on the scale or rubric depicting student status on the learning goal.

☐ Teacher charts the progress of the entire class on the learning goal.

Student Evidence

☐ When asked, students can describe their status relative to the learning goal using the scale or rubric.

☐ Students systematically update their status on the learning goal.

Scale

	Innovating (4)	Applying (3)	Developing (2)	Beginning (1)	Not Using (0)
Tracking student progress	Adapts and creates new strategies for unique student needs and situations	Facilitates tracking of student progress using a formative approach to assessment, and monitors the extent to which students understand their level of performance	Facilitates tracking of student progress using a formative approach to assessment	Uses strategy incorrectly or with parts missing	Strategy was called for but not exhibited

3. Celebrating Student Success

The teacher provides students with recognition of their current status and their knowledge gain relative to the learning goal.	*Notes*

Teacher Evidence

☐ Teacher acknowledges students who have achieved a certain score on the scale or rubric.

☐ Teacher acknowledges students who have made gains in their knowledge and skill relative to the learning goal.

☐ Teacher acknowledges and celebrates the final status and progress of the entire class.

☐ Teacher uses a variety of ways to celebrate success.
- Show of hands
- Certification of success
- Parent notification
- Round of applause

Student Evidence

☐ Students show signs of pride regarding their accomplishments in the class.

☐ When asked, students say they want to continue to make progress.

Scale

	Innovating (4)	Applying (3)	Developing (2)	Beginning (1)	Not Using (0)
Celebrating student success	Adapts and creates new strategies for unique student needs and situations	Provides students with recognition of their current status and their knowledge gain relative to the learning goal, and monitors the extent to which students are motivated to enhance their status	Provides students with recognition of their current status and their knowledge gain relative to the learning goal	Uses strategy incorrectly or with parts missing	Strategy was called for but not exhibited

Design Question 6: **What will I do to establish and maintain classroom rules and procedures?**

4. Establishing Classroom Routines

The teacher reviews expectations regarding rules and procedures to ensure their effective execution.	*Notes*

Teacher Evidence	**Student Evidence**
☐ Teacher involves students in designing classroom routines.	☐ Students follow clear routines during class.
☐ Teacher uses classroom meetings to review and process rules and procedures.	☐ When asked, students can describe established rules and procedures.
☐ Teacher reminds students of rules and procedures.	☐ When asked, students describe the classroom as an orderly place.
☐ Teacher asks students to restate or explain rules and procedures.	☐ Students recognize cues and signals by the teacher.
☐ Teacher provides cues or signals when a rule or procedure should be used.	☐ Students regulate their own behavior.

Scale					
	Innovating (4)	**Applying (3)**	**Developing (2)**	**Beginning (1)**	**Not Using (0)**
Establishing classroom routines	Adapts and creates new strategies for unique student needs and situations	Establishes and reviews expectations regarding rules and procedures, and monitors the extent to which students understand the rules and procedures	Establishes and reviews expectations regarding rules and procedures	Uses strategy incorrectly or with parts missing	Strategy was called for but not exhibited

5. Organizing the Physical Layout of the Classroom for Learning

The teacher organizes the physical layout of the classroom to facilitate movement and focus on learning.

Notes

Teacher Evidence

☐ The physical layout of the classroom has clear traffic patterns.

☐ The physical layout of the classroom provides easy access to material and centers.

☐ The classroom is decorated in a way that enhances student learning:
- Bulletin boards relate to current content.
- Student work is displayed.

Student Evidence

☐ Students move easily about the classroom.

☐ Students make use of materials and learning centers.

☐ Students attend to examples of their work that are displayed.

☐ Students attend to information on the bulletin boards.

☐ Students can easily focus on instruction.

Scale

	Innovating (4)	Applying (3)	Developing (2)	Beginning (1)	Not Using (0)
Organizing the physical layout of the classroom for learning	Adapts and creates new strategies for unique student needs and situations	Organizes the physical layout of the classroom to facilitate movement and focus on learning, and monitors the impact of the environment on student learning	Organizes the physical layout of the classroom to facilitate movement and focus on learning	Uses strategy incorrectly or with parts missing	Strategy was called for but not exhibited

© 2011 Robert J. Marzano

LESSON SEGMENTS ADDRESSING CONTENT

Design Question 2: **What will I do to help students effectively interact with new knowledge?**

1. Identifying Critical Information	
The teacher identifies a lesson or part of a lesson as involving important information to which students should pay particular attention.	*Notes*

Teacher Evidence	Student Evidence
☐ Teacher begins the lesson by explaining why upcoming content is important.	☐ When asked, students can describe the level of importance of the information addressed in class.
☐ Teacher tells students to get ready for some important information.	☐ When asked, students can explain why the content is important to pay attention to.
☐ Teacher cues the importance of upcoming information in some indirect fashion. • Tone of voice • Body position • Level of excitement	☐ Students visibly adjust their level of engagement.

Scale

	Innovating (4)	Applying (3)	Developing (2)	Beginning (1)	Not Using (0)
Identifying critical information	Adapts and creates new strategies for unique student needs and situations	Signals to students which content is critical versus noncritical, and monitors the extent to which students are attending to critical information	Signals to students which content is critical versus noncritical	Uses strategy incorrectly or with parts missing	Strategy was called for but not exhibited

2. Organizing Students to Interact with New Knowledge

The teacher organizes students into small groups to facilitate the processing of new information.	*Notes*

Teacher Evidence

☐ Teacher has established routines for student grouping and student interaction in groups.

☐ Teacher organizes students into ad hoc groups for the lesson.
- Dyads
- Triads
- Small groups up to about five

Student Evidence

☐ Students move to groups in an orderly fashion.

☐ Students appear to understand expectations about appropriate behavior in groups.
- Respect opinions of others
- Add their perspective to discussions
- Ask and answer questions

Scale

	Innovating (4)	Applying (3)	Developing (2)	Beginning (1)	Not Using (0)
Organizing students to interact with new knowledge	Adapts and creates new strategies for unique student needs and situations	Organizes students into small groups to facilitate the processing of new knowledge, and monitors group processing	Organizes students into small groups to facilitate the processing of new knowledge	Uses strategy incorrectly or with parts missing	Strategy was called for but not exhibited

3. Previewing New Content

The teacher engages students in activities that help them link what they already know to the new content about to be addressed and facilitates these linkages.	*Notes*

Teacher Evidence

☐ Teacher uses preview question before reading.

☐ Teacher uses K-W-L strategy or variation of it.

☐ Teacher asks or reminds students what they already know about the topic.

☐ Teacher provides an advanced organizer.
- Outline
- Graphic organizer

☐ Teacher has students brainstorm.

☐ Teacher uses anticipation guide.

☐ Teacher uses motivational hook/launching activity.
- Anecdotes
- Short selection from video

☐ Teacher uses word splash activity to connect vocabulary to upcoming content.

Student Evidence

☐ When asked, students can explain linkages with prior knowledge.

☐ When asked, students make predictions about upcoming content.

☐ When asked, students can provide a purpose for what they are about to learn.

☐ Students actively engage in previewing activities.

Scale

	Innovating (4)	Applying (3)	Developing (2)	Beginning (1)	Not Using (0)
Previewing new content	Adapts and creates new strategies for unique student needs and situations	Engages students in learning activities that require them to preview and link new knowledge to what has been addressed, and monitors the extent to which students are making linkages	Engages students in learning activities that require them to preview and link new knowledge to what has been addressed	Uses strategy incorrectly or with parts missing	Strategy was called for but not exhibited

4. Chunking Content into "Digestible Bites"

Based on student needs, the teacher breaks the content into small chunks (i.e., digestible bites) of information that can be easily processed by students.	*Notes*

Teacher Evidence

☐ Teacher stops at strategic points in a verbal presentation.

☐ While playing a videotape, the teacher turns the tape off at key junctures.

☐ While providing a demonstration, the teacher stops at strategic points.

☐ While students are reading information or stories orally as a class, the teacher stops at strategic points.

Student Evidence

☐ When asked, students can explain why the teacher is stopping at various points.

☐ Students appear to know what is expected of them when the teacher stops at strategic points.

Scale

	Innovating (4)	Applying (3)	Developing (2)	Beginning (1)	Not Using (0)
Chunking content into "digestible bites"	Adapts and creates new strategies for unique student needs and situations	Breaks input experiences into small chunks based on student needs, and monitors the extent to which chunks are appropriate	Breaks input experiences into small chunks based on student needs	Uses strategy incorrectly or with parts missing	Strategy was called for but not exhibited

5. Group Processing of New Information

During breaks in the presentation of content, the teacher engages students in actively processing new information.

Notes

Teacher Evidence

☐ Teacher has group members summarize new information.

☐ Teacher employs formal group processing strategies.
- Jigsaw
- Reciprocal teaching
- Concept attainment

Student Evidence

☐ When asked, students can explain what they have just learned.

☐ Students volunteer predictions.

☐ Students voluntarily ask clarification questions.

☐ Groups are actively discussing the content.
- Group members ask each other and answer questions about the information.
- Group members make predictions about what they expect next.

Scale

	Innovating (4)	Applying (3)	Developing (2)	Beginning (1)	Not Using (0)
Group processing of new information	Adapts and creates new strategies for unique student needs and situations	Engages students in summarizing, predicting, and questioning activities; and monitors the extent to which the activities enhance students' understanding	Engages students in summarizing, predicting, and questioning activities	Uses strategy incorrectly or with parts missing	Strategy was called for but not exhibited

6. Elaborating on New Information

The teacher asks questions or engages students in activities that require elaborative inferences that go beyond what was explicitly taught.	Notes

Teacher Evidence

☐ Teacher asks explicit questions that require students to make elaborative inferences about the content.

☐ Teacher asks students to explain and defend their inferences.

☐ Teacher presents situations or problems that require inferences.

Student Evidence

☐ Students volunteer answers to inferential questions.

☐ Students provide explanations and "proofs" for inferences.

Scale

	Innovating (4)	Applying (3)	Developing (2)	Beginning (1)	Not Using (0)
Elaborating on new information	Adapts and creates new strategies for unique student needs and situations	Engages students in answering inferential questions, and monitors the extent to which students elaborate on what was explicitly taught	Engages students in answering inferential questions	Uses strategy incorrectly or with parts missing	Strategy was called for but not exhibited

7. Recording and Representing Knowledge	
The teacher engages students in activities that help them record their understanding of new content in linguistic ways and/or represent the content in nonlinguistic ways.	Notes

Teacher Evidence

☐ Teacher asks students to summarize the information they have learned.

☐ Teacher asks students to generate notes that identify critical information in the content.

☐ Teacher asks students to create nonlinguistic representations for new content.
- Graphic organizers
- Pictures
- Pictographs
- Flow charts

☐ Teacher asks students to create mnemonics that organize the content.

Student Evidence

☐ Students' summaries and notes include critical content.

☐ Students' nonlinguistic representations include critical content.

☐ When asked, students can explain main points of the lesson.

Scale

	Innovating (4)	Applying (3)	Developing (2)	Beginning (1)	Not Using (0)
Recording and representing knowledge	Adapts and creates new strategies for unique student needs and situations	Engages students in activities that help them record their understanding of new content in linguistic ways and/or in nonlinguistic ways, and monitors the extent to which this enhances students' understanding	Engages students in activities that help them record their understanding of new content in linguistic ways and/or in nonlinguistic ways	Uses strategy incorrectly or with parts missing	Strategy was called for but not exhibited

8. Reflecting on Learning

The teacher engages students in activities that help them reflect on their learning and the learning process.	*Notes*

Teacher Evidence

☐ Teacher asks students to state or record what they are clear about and what they are confused about.

☐ Teacher asks students to state or record how hard they tried.

☐ Teacher asks students to state or record what they might have done to enhance their learning.

Student Evidence

☐ When asked, students can explain what they are clear about and what they are confused about.

☐ When asked, students can describe how hard they tried.

☐ When asked, students can explain what they could have done to enhance their learning.

Scale

	Innovating (4)	Applying (3)	Developing (2)	Beginning (1)	Not Using (0)
Reflecting on learning	Adapts and creates new strategies for unique student needs and situations	Engages students in reflecting on their own learning and the learning process, and monitors the extent to which students self-assess their understanding and effort	Engages students in reflecting on their own learning and the learning process	Uses strategy incorrectly or with parts missing	Strategy was called for but not exhibited

Design Question 3: What will I do to help students practice and deepen their understanding of new knowledge?

9. Reviewing Content	
The teacher engages students in a brief review of content that highlights the critical information.	*Notes*

Teacher Evidence

☐ Teacher begins the lesson with a brief review of content.

☐ Teacher uses specific strategies to review information.
- Summary
- Problem that must be solved using previous information
- Questions that require a review of content
- Demonstration
- Brief practice test or exercise

Student Evidence

☐ When asked, students can describe the previous content on which new lesson is based.

☐ Student responses to class activities indicate that they recall previous content.

Scale

	Innovating (4)	Applying (3)	Developing (2)	Beginning (1)	Not Using (0)
Reviewing content	Adapts and creates new strategies for unique student needs and situations	Engages students in a brief review of content that highlights the critical information, and monitors the extent to which students can recall and describe previous content	Engages students in a brief review of content that highlights the critical information	Uses strategy incorrectly or with parts missing	Strategy was called for but not exhibited

10. Organizing Students to Practice and Deepen Knowledge

The teacher uses grouping in ways that facilitate practicing and deepening knowledge.	*Notes*

Teacher Evidence

☐ Teacher organizes students into groups with the expressed idea of deepening their knowledge of informational content.

☐ Teacher organizes students into groups with the expressed idea of practicing a skill, strategy, or process.

Student Evidence

☐ When asked, students explain how the group work supports their learning.

☐ While in groups, students interact in explicit ways to deepen their knowledge of informational content or practice a skill, strategy, or process.
• Asking each other questions
• Obtaining feedback from their peers

Scale

	Innovating (4)	Applying (3)	Developing (2)	Beginning (1)	Not Using (0)
Organizing students to practice and deepen knowledge	Adapts and creates new strategies for unique student needs and situations	Organizes students into groups to practice and deepen their knowledge, and monitors the extent to which the group work extends their learning	Organizes students into groups to practice and deepen their knowledge	Uses strategy incorrectly or with parts missing	Strategy was called for but not exhibited

11. Using Homework

When appropriate (as opposed to routinely), the teacher designs homework to deepen students' knowledge of informational content or to practice a skill, strategy, or process.	*Notes*

Teacher Evidence

☐ Teacher communicates a clear purpose for homework.

☐ Teacher extends an activity that was begun in class to provide students with more time.

☐ Teacher assigns a well-crafted homework assignment that allows students to practice and deepen their knowledge independently.

Student Evidence

☐ When asked, students can describe how the homework assignment will deepen their understanding of informational content or help them practice a skill, strategy, or process.

☐ Students ask clarifying questions of the homework that help them understand its purpose.

Scale

	Innovating (4)	Applying (3)	Developing (2)	Beginning (1)	Not Using (0)
Using homework	Adapts and creates new strategies for unique student needs and situations	When appropriate (as opposed to routinely), assigns homework that is designed to deepen knowledge of information or to practice a skill, strategy, or process; and monitors the extent to which students understand the homework	When appropriate (as opposed to routinely), assigns homework that is designed to deepen knowledge of information or to practice a skill, strategy, or process	Uses strategy incorrectly or with parts missing	Strategy was called for but not exhibited

© 2011 Robert J. Marzano

12. Examining Similarities and Differences

When the content is informational, the teacher helps students deepen their knowledge by examining similarities and differences.	*Notes*

Teacher Evidence

☐ Teacher engages students in activities that require students to examine similarities and differences between content.
- Comparison activities
- Classifying activities
- Analogy activities
- Metaphor activities

☐ Teacher facilitates the use of these activities to help students deepen their understanding of content.
- Asking students to summarize what they have learned from the activity
- Asking students to explain how the activity has added to their understanding

Student Evidence

☐ Student artifacts indicate that their knowledge has been extended as a result of the activity.

☐ When asked about the activity, student responses indicate that they have deepened their understanding.

☐ When asked, students can explain similarities and differences.

☐ Student artifacts indicate that they can identify similarities and differences.

Scale

	Innovating (4)	Applying (3)	Developing (2)	Beginning (1)	Not Using (0)
Examining similarities and differences	Adapts and creates new strategies for unique student needs and situations	When content is informational, engages students in activities that require them to examine similarities and differences, and monitors the extent to which the students are deepening their knowledge	When content is informational, engages students in activities that require them to examine similarities and differences	Uses strategy incorrectly or with parts missing	Strategy was called for but not exhibited

© 2011 Robert J. Marzano

13. Examining Errors in Reasoning

When content is informational, the teacher helps students deepen their knowledge by examining their own reasoning or the logic of the information as presented to them.	*Notes*

Teacher Evidence

☐ Teacher asks students to examine information for errors or informal fallacies.
- Faulty logic
- Attacks
- Weak reference
- Misinformation

☐ Teacher asks students to examine the strength of support presented for a claim.
- Statement of a clear claim
- Evidence for the claim presented
- Qualifiers presented showing exceptions to the claim

Student Evidence

☐ When asked, students can describe errors or informal fallacies in information.

☐ When asked, students can explain the overall structure of an argument presented to support a claim.

☐ Student artifacts indicate that they can identify errors in reasoning.

Scale

	Innovating (4)	Applying (3)	Developing (2)	Beginning (1)	Not Using (0)
Examining errors in reasoning	Adapts and creates new strategies for unique student needs and situations	When content is informational, engages students in activities that require them to examine their own reasoning or the logic of information as presented to them, and monitors the extent to which students are deepening their knowledge	When content is informational, engages students in activities that require them to examine their own reasoning or the logic of information as presented to them	Uses strategy incorrectly or with parts missing	Strategy was called for but not exhibited

14. Practicing Skills, Strategies, and Processes

When the content involves a skill, strategy, or process, the teacher engages students in practice activities that help them develop fluency.	*Notes*

Teacher Evidence

☐ Teacher engages students in massed and distributed practice activities that are appropriate to their current ability to execute a skill, strategy, or process.
• Guided practice if students cannot perform the skill, strategy, or process independently
• Independent practice if students can perform the skill, strategy, or process independently

Student Evidence

☐ Students perform the skill, strategy, or process with increased confidence.

☐ Students perform the skill, strategy, or process with increased competence.

Scale					
	Innovating (4)	**Applying (3)**	**Developing (2)**	**Beginning (1)**	**Not Using (0)**
Practicing skills, strategies, and processes	Adapts and creates new strategies for unique student needs and situations	When content involves a skill, strategy, or process, engages students in practice activities, and monitors the extent to which the practice is increasing student fluency	When content involves a skill, strategy, or process, engages students in practice activities	Uses strategy incorrectly or with parts missing	Strategy was called for but not exhibited

15. Revising Knowledge

The teacher engages students in revision of previous knowledge about content addressed in previous lessons.

Notes

Teacher Evidence

☐ Teacher asks students to examine previous entries in their academic notebooks or notes.

☐ Teacher engages the whole class in an examination of how the current lesson changed perceptions and understandings of previous content.

☐ Teacher has students explain how their understanding has changed.

Student Evidence

☐ Students make corrections to information previously recorded about content.

☐ When asked, students can explain previous errors or misconceptions they had about content.

Scale

	Innovating (4)	Applying (3)	Developing (2)	Beginning (1)	Not Using (0)
Revising knowledge	Adapts and creates new strategies for unique student needs and situations	Engages students in revision of previous content, and monitors the extent to which these revisions deepen students' understanding	Engages students in revision of previous content	Uses strategy incorrectly or with parts missing	Strategy was called for but not exhibited

Design Question 4: **What will I do to help students generate and test hypotheses about new knowledge?**

16. Organizing Students for Cognitively Complex Tasks	
The teacher organizes the class in such a way as to facilitate students working on complex tasks that require them to generate and test hypotheses.	*Notes*

Teacher Evidence

☐ Teacher establishes the need to generate and test hypotheses.

☐ Teacher organizes students into groups to generate and test hypotheses.

Student Evidence

☐ When asked, students describe the importance of generating and testing hypotheses about content.

☐ When asked, students explain how groups support their learning.

☐ Students use group activities to help them generate and test hypotheses.

Scale

	Innovating (4)	Applying (3)	Developing (2)	Beginning (1)	Not Using (0)
Organizing students for cognitively complex tasks	Adapts and creates new strategies for unique student needs and situations	Organizes students into groups to facilitate working on cognitively complex tasks, and monitors the extent to which group processes facilitate generating and testing hypotheses	Organizes students into groups to facilitate working on cognitively complex tasks	Uses strategy incorrectly or with parts missing	Strategy was called for but not exhibited

© 2011 Robert J. Marzano

17. Engaging Students in Cognitively Complex Tasks Involving Hypothesis Generating and Testing

The teacher engages students in complex tasks (e.g., decision making, problem solving, experimental inquiry, investigation) that require them to generate and test hypotheses.	*Notes*

Teacher Evidence

☐ Teacher engages students with an explicit decision making, problem solving, experimental inquiry, or investigation task that requires them to generate and test hypotheses.

☐ Teacher facilitates students generating their own individual or group task that requires them to generate and test hypotheses.

Student Evidence

☐ Students are clearly working on tasks that require them to generate and test hypotheses.

☐ When asked, students can explain the hypothesis they are testing.

☐ When asked, students can explain whether their hypothesis was confirmed or disconfirmed.

☐ Student artifacts indicate that they can engage in decision making, problem solving, experiential inquiry, or investigation.

Scale

	Innovating (4)	Applying (3)	Developing (2)	Beginning (1)	Not Using (0)
Engaging students in cognitively complex tasks involving hypothesis generating and testing	Adapts and creates new strategies for unique student needs and situations	Engages students in cognitively complex tasks (e.g., decision making, problem solving, experimental inquiry, investigation), and monitors the extent to which students are generating and testing hypotheses	Engages students in cognitively complex tasks (e.g., decision making, problem solving, experimental inquiry, investigation)	Uses strategy incorrectly or with parts missing	Strategy was called for but not exhibited

18. Providing Resources and Guidance

The teacher acts as resource provider and guide as students engage in cognitively complex tasks.	*Notes*

Teacher Evidence

☐ Teacher makes him- or herself available to students who need guidance or resources.
- Circulates around the room
- Provides easy access to him- or herself

☐ Teacher interacts with students during the class to determine their needs for hypothesis generation and testing tasks.

☐ Teacher volunteers resources and guidance as needed by the entire class, groups of students, or individual students.

Student Evidence

☐ Students seek out the teacher for advice and guidance regarding hypothesis generation and testing tasks.

☐ When asked, students can explain how the teacher provides assistance and guidance in hypothesis generation and testing tasks.

Scale

	Innovating (4)	Applying (3)	Developing (2)	Beginning (1)	Not Using (0)
Providing resources and guidance	Adapts and creates new strategies for unique student needs and situations	Acts as a guide and resource provider as students engage in cognitively complex tasks, and monitors the extent to which students request and use guidance and resources	Acts as a guide and resource provider as students engage in cognitively complex tasks	Uses strategy incorrectly or with parts missing	Strategy was called for but not exhibited

LESSON SEGMENTS ENACTED ON THE SPOT

Design Question 5: What will I do to engage students?

1. Noticing and Reacting When Students Are Not Engaged	
The teacher scans the room making note of when students are not engaged and takes overt action.	*Notes*

Teacher Evidence

☐ Teacher notices when specific students or groups of students are not engaged.

☐ Teacher notices when the energy level in the room is low.

☐ Teacher takes action to reengage students.

Student Evidence

☐ Students appear aware of the fact that the teacher is taking note of their level of engagement.

☐ Students try to increase their level of engagement when prompted.

☐ When asked, students explain that the teacher expects high levels of engagement.

Scale

	Innovating (4)	Applying (3)	Developing (2)	Beginning (1)	Not Using (0)
Noticing and reacting when students are not engaged	Adapts and creates new strategies for unique student needs and situations	Scans the room making note of when students are not engaged, takes action, and monitors the extent to which students re-engage	Scans the room making note of when students are not engaged and takes action	Uses strategy incorrectly or with parts missing	Strategy was called for but not exhibited

© 2011 Robert J. Marzano

2. Using Academic Games

The teacher uses academic games and inconsequential competition to maintain student engagement.	*Notes*

Teacher Evidence

☐ Teacher uses structured games such as Jeopardy, Family Feud, and the like.

☐ Teacher develops impromptu games such as making a game out of which answer might be correct for a given question.

☐ Teacher uses friendly competition along with classroom games.

Student Evidence

☐ Students engage in the games with some enthusiasm.

☐ When asked, students can explain how the games keep their interest and help them learn or remember content.

Scale					
	Innovating (4)	**Applying (3)**	**Developing (2)**	**Beginning (1)**	**Not Using (0)**
Using academic games	Adapts and creates new strategies for unique student needs and situations	Uses academic games and inconsequential competition to maintain student engagement, and monitors the extent to which students focus on the academic content of the game	Uses academic games and inconsequential competition to maintain student engagement	Uses strategy incorrectly or with parts missing	Strategy was called for but not exhibited

3. Managing Response Rates During Questioning

The teacher uses response rates techniques to maintain student engagement in answering questions.	*Notes*

Teacher Evidence

☐ Teacher uses wait time.

☐ Teacher uses response cards.

☐ Teacher has students use hand signals to respond to questions.

☐ Teacher uses choral response.

☐ Teacher uses technology to keep track of students' responses.

☐ Teacher uses response chaining.

Student Evidence

☐ Multiple students or the entire class responds to questions posed by the teacher.

☐ When asked, students can describe their thinking about specific questions posed by the teacher.

Scale

	Innovating (4)	Applying (3)	Developing (2)	Beginning (1)	Not Using (0)
Managing response rates during questioning	Adapts and creates new strategies for unique student needs and situations	Uses response rate techniques to maintain student engagement in answering questions, and monitors the extent to which the techniques keep students engaged	Uses response rate techniques to maintain student engagement in answering questions	Uses strategy incorrectly or with parts missing	Strategy was called for but not exhibited

© 2011 Robert J. Marzano

4. Using Physical Movement

The teacher uses physical movement to maintain student engagement.	*Notes*

Teacher Evidence

☐ Teacher has students stand up and stretch or do related activities when their energy is low.

☐ Teacher uses activities that require students to physically move to respond to questions.
• Voting with your feet
• Going to the part of the room that represents the answer you agree with

☐ Teacher has students physically act out or model content to increase energy and engagement.

☐ Teacher use give-one-get-one activities that require students to move about the room.

Student Evidence

☐ Students engage in the physical activities designed by the teacher.

☐ When asked, students can explain how the physical movement keeps their interest and helps them learn.

Scale					
	Innovating (4)	**Applying (3)**	**Developing (2)**	**Beginning (1)**	**Not Using (0)**
Using physical movement	Adapts and creates new strategies for unique student needs and situations	Uses physical movement to maintain student engagement, and monitors the extent to which these activities enhance student engagement	Uses physical movement to maintain student engagement	Uses strategy incorrectly or with parts missing	Strategy was called for but not exhibited

5. Maintaining a Lively Pace

The teacher uses pacing techniques to maintain students' engagement.	*Notes*

Teacher Evidence

☐ Teacher employs crisp transitions from one activity to another.

☐ Teacher alters pace appropriately (i.e., speeds up and slows down).

Student Evidence

☐ Students quickly adapt to transitions and reengage when a new activity is started.

☐ When asked about the pace of the class. students describe it as not too fast or not too slow.

Scale

	Innovating (4)	Applying (3)	Developing (2)	Beginning (1)	Not Using (0)
Maintaining a lively pace	Adapts and creates new strategies for unique student needs and situations	Uses pacing techniques to maintain students' engagement, and monitors the extent to which these techniques keep students engaged	Uses pacing techniques to maintain students' engagement	Uses strategy incorrectly or with parts missing	Strategy was called for but not exhibited

6. Demonstrating Intensity and Enthusiasm	
The teacher demonstrates intensity and enthusiasm for the content in a variety of ways.	*Notes*

Teacher Evidence

☐ Teacher describes personal experiences that relate to the content.

☐ Teacher signals excitement for content.
- Physical gestures
- Voice tone
- Dramatization of information

☐ Teacher overtly adjusts energy level.

Student Evidence

☐ When asked, students say that the teacher "likes the content" and "likes teaching."

☐ Students' attention levels increase when the teacher demonstrates enthusiasm and intensity for the content.

Scale

	Innovating (4)	Applying (3)	Developing (2)	Beginning (1)	Not Using (0)
Demonstrating intensity and enthusiasm	Adapts and creates new strategies for unique student needs and situations	Demonstrates intensity and enthusiasm for the content in a variety of ways, and monitors the extent to which students' engagement increases	Demonstrates intensity and enthusiasm for the content in a variety of ways	Uses strategy incorrectly or with parts missing	Strategy was called for but not exhibited

© 2011 Robert J. Marzano

7. Using Friendly Controversy

The teacher uses friendly controversy techniques to maintain student engagement.

Notes

Teacher Evidence

☐ Teacher structures mini-debates about the content.

☐ Teacher has students examine multiple perspectives and opinions about the content.

☐ Teacher elicits different opinions on content from members of the class.

Student Evidence

☐ Students engage in friendly controversy activities with enhanced engagement.

☐ When asked, students describe friendly controversy activities as "stimulating," "fun," and so on.

☐ When asked, students explain how a friendly controversy activity helped them better understand the content.

Scale

	Innovating (4)	Applying (3)	Developing (2)	Beginning (1)	Not Using (0)
Using friendly controversy	Adapts and creates new strategies for unique student needs and situations	Uses friendly controversy techniques to maintain student engagement, and monitors the effect on student engagement	Uses friendly controversy techniques to maintain student engagement	Uses strategy incorrectly or with parts missing	Strategy was called for but not exhibited

8. Providing Opportunities for Students to Talk About Themselves

The teacher provides students with opportunities to relate what is being addressed in class to their personal interests.	*Notes*

Teacher Evidence

☐ Teacher is aware of student interests and makes connections between these interests and class content.

☐ Teacher structures activities that ask students to make connections between the content and their personal interests.

☐ When students are explaining how content relates to their personal interests, the teacher appears encouraging and interested.

Student Evidence

☐ Students engage in activities that require them to make connections between their personal interests and the content.

☐ When asked, students explain how making connections between content and their personal interests engages them and helps them better understand the content.

Scale

	Innovating (4)	Applying (3)	Developing (2)	Beginning (1)	Not Using (0)
Providing opportunities for students to talk about themselves	Adapts and creates new strategies for unique student needs and situations	Provides students with opportunities to relate what is being addressed in class to their personal interests, and monitors the extent to which these activities enhance student engagement	Provides students with opportunities to relate what is being addressed in class to their personal interests	Uses strategy incorrectly or with parts missing	Strategy was called for but not exhibited

9. Presenting Unusual or Intriguing Information

The teacher uses unusual or intriguing information about the content in a manner that enhances student engagement.

Notes

Teacher Evidence

☐ Teacher systematically provides interesting facts and details about the content.

☐ Teacher encourages students to identify interesting information about the content.

☐ Teacher engages students in activities like "Believe It or Not" about the content.

☐ Teacher uses guest speakers to provide unusual information about the content.

☐ Teacher tells stories that are related to the content.

Student Evidence

☐ Students' attention increases when unusual information is presented about the content.

☐ When asked, students explain how the unusual information makes them more interested in the content.

Scale

	Innovating (4)	Applying (3)	Developing (2)	Beginning (1)	Not Using (0)
Presenting unusual or intriguing information	Adapts and creates new strategies for unique student needs and situations	Uses unusual or intriguing information about the content, and monitors the extent to which this information enhances students' interest in the content	Uses unusual or intriguing information about the content	Uses strategy incorrectly or with parts missing	Strategy was called for but not exhibited

Design Question 7: What will I do to recognize and acknowledge adherence or lack of adherence to classroom rules and procedures?

10. Demonstrating "Withitness"	
The teacher uses behaviors associated with "withitness" to maintain adherence to rules and procedures.	*Notes*

Teacher Evidence

☐ Teacher physically occupies all quadrants of the room.

☐ Teacher scans the entire room, making eye contact with all students.

☐ Teacher recognizes potential sources of disruption and deals with them immediately.

☐ Teacher proactively addresses inflammatory situations.

Student Evidence

☐ Students recognize that the teacher is aware of their behavior.

☐ When asked, students describe the teacher as "aware of what is going on" or "has eyes on the back of his/her head."

Scale

	Innovating (4)	Applying (3)	Developing (2)	Beginning (1)	Not Using (0)
Demonstrating "withitness"	Adapts and creates new strategies for unique student needs and situations	Uses behaviors associated with "withitness," and monitors the effect on students' behavior	Uses behaviors associated with "withitness"	Uses strategy incorrectly or with parts missing	Strategy was called for but not exhibited

11. Applying Consequences	
The teacher applies consequences for not following rules and procedures consistently and fairly.	*Notes*

Teacher Evidence

☐ Teacher provides nonverbal signals when students' behavior is not appropriate.
- Eye contact
- Proximity
- Tapping on the desk
- Shaking head "no"

☐ Teacher provides verbal signals when students' behavior is not appropriate.
- Telling students to stop
- Telling students that their behavior violates a rule or procedure

☐ Teacher uses group contingency consequences when appropriate (i.e., whole group must demonstrate a specific behavior).

☐ Teacher involves the home when appropriate (i.e., makes a call home to parents to help extinguish inappropriate behavior).

☐ Teacher uses direct cost consequences when appropriate (e.g., student must fix something he or she has broken).

Student Evidence

☐ Students cease inappropriate behavior when signaled by the teacher.

☐ Students accept consequences as part of the way class is conducted.

☐ When asked, students describe the teacher as fair in application of rules.

Scale

	Innovating (4)	Applying (3)	Developing (2)	Beginning (1)	Not Using (0)
Applying consequences	Adapts and creates new strategies for unique student needs and situations	Applies consequences for not following rules and procedures consistently and fairly, and monitors the extent to which rules and procedures are followed	Applies consequences for not following rules and procedures consistently and fairly	Uses strategy incorrectly or with parts missing	Strategy was called for but not exhibited

12. Acknowledging Adherence to Rules and Procedures	
The teacher consistently and fairly acknowledges adherence to rules and procedures.	*Notes*

Teacher Evidence	Student Evidence
☐ Teacher provides nonverbal signals that a rule or procedure has been followed. • Smile • Nod of head • High five ☐ Teacher gives verbal cues that a rule or procedure has been followed. • Thanking students for following a rule or procedure • Describing student behaviors that adhere to rule or procedure ☐ Teacher notifies the home when a rule or procedure has been followed. ☐ Teacher uses tangible recognition when a rule or procedure has been followed. • Certificate of merit • Token economies	☐ Students appear appreciative of the teacher acknowledging their positive behavior. ☐ When asked, students describe teacher as appreciative of their good behavior. ☐ The number of students adhering to rules and procedures increases.

Scale

	Innovating (4)	Applying (3)	Developing (2)	Beginning (1)	Not Using (0)
Acknowledging adherence to rules and procedures	Adapts and creates new strategies for unique student needs and situations	Acknowledges adherence to rules and procedures consistently and fairly, and monitors the extent to which these actions affect students' behavior	Acknowledges adherence to rules and procedures consistently and fairly	Uses strategy incorrectly or with parts missing	Strategy was called for but not exhibited

Design Question 8: **What will I do to establish and maintain effective relationships with students?**

13. Understanding Students' Interests and Background	
The teacher uses students' interests and background to produce a climate of acceptance and community.	*Notes*

Teacher Evidence	**Student Evidence**
☐ Teacher has side discussions with students about events in their lives.	☐ When asked, students describe the teacher as someone who knows them and/or is interested in them.
☐ Teacher has discussions with students about topics in which they are interested.	☐ Students respond when the teacher demonstrates understanding of their interests and background.
☐ Teacher builds student interests into lessons.	☐ When asked, students say they feel accepted.

Scale

	Innovating (4)	Applying (3)	Developing (2)	Beginning (1)	Not Using (0)
Understanding students' interests and background	Adapts and creates new strategies for unique student needs and situations	Uses students' interests and background during interactions with students, and monitors the sense of community in the classroom	Uses students' interests and background during interactions with students	Uses strategy incorrectly or with parts missing	Strategy was called for but not exhibited

© 2011 Robert J. Marzano

14. Using Behaviors that Indicate Affection for Students

When appropriate, the teacher uses verbal and nonverbal behavior that indicates caring for students.

Notes

Teacher Evidence

☐ Teacher compliments students regarding academic and personal accomplishments.

☐ Teacher engages in informal conversations with students that are not related to academics.

☐ Teacher uses humor with students when appropriate.

☐ Teacher smiles, nods, and so forth, at students when appropriate.

☐ Teacher puts hand on students' shoulders when appropriate.

Student Evidence

☐ When asked, students describe the teacher as someone who cares for them.

☐ Students respond to the teacher's verbal interactions.

☐ Students respond to the teacher's nonverbal interactions.

Scale

	Innovating (4)	Applying (3)	Developing (2)	Beginning (1)	Not Using (0)
Using behaviors that indicate affection for students	Adapts and creates new strategies for unique student needs and situations	Uses verbal and nonverbal behaviors that indicate caring for students, and monitors the quality of relationships in the classroom	Uses verbal and nonverbal behaviors that indicate caring for students	Uses strategy incorrectly or with parts missing	Strategy was called for but not exhibited

15. Displaying Objectivity and Control

The teacher behaves in an objective and controlled manner.

Notes

Teacher Evidence

☐ Teacher does not exhibit extremes in positive or negative emotions.

☐ Teacher addresses inflammatory issues and events in a calm and controlled manner.

☐ Teacher interacts with all students in the same calm and controlled fashion.

☐ Teacher does not demonstrate personal offense at student misbehavior.

Student Evidence

☐ Students are settled by the teacher's calm demeanor.

☐ When asked, the students describe the teacher as in control of him- or herself and in control of the class.

☐ When asked, students say that the teacher does not hold grudges or take things personally.

Scale

	Innovating (4)	Applying (3)	Developing (2)	Beginning (1)	Not Using (0)
Displaying objectivity and control	Adapts and creates new strategies for unique student needs and situations	Behaves in an objective and controlled manner, and monitors the effect on the classroom climate	Behaves in an objective and controlled manner	Uses strategy incorrectly or with parts missing	Strategy was called for but not exhibited

Design Question 9: What will I do to communicate high expectations for all students?

16. Demonstrating Value and Respect for Low-Expectancy Students

The teacher exhibits behaviors that demonstrate value and respect for low-expectancy students.	*Notes*

Teacher Evidence	**Student Evidence**
☐ When asked, the teacher can identify the students for whom there have been low expectations and the various ways in which these students have been treated differently from high-expectancy students. ☐ The teacher provides low-expectancy students with nonverbal indications that they are valued and respected. • Eye contact • Smile • Appropriate physical contact ☐ The teacher provides low-expectancy students with verbal indications that they are valued and respected. • Playful dialogue • Addressing students in a manner they view as respectful ☐ Teacher does not allow negative comments about low-expectancy students.	☐ When asked, students say that the teacher cares for all students. ☐ Students treat each other with respect.

Scale

	Innovating (4)	Applying (3)	Developing (2)	Beginning (1)	Not Using (0)
Demonstrating value and respect for low-expectancy students	Adapts and creates new strategies for unique student needs and situations	Exhibits behaviors that demonstrate value and respect for low-expectancy students, and monitors the impact on low-expectancy students	Exhibits behaviors that demonstrate value and respect for low-expectancy students	Uses strategy incorrectly or with parts missing	Strategy was called for but not exhibited

17. Asking Questions of Low-Expectancy Students

The teacher asks questions of low-expectancy students with the same frequency and depth as with high-expectancy students.

Notes

Teacher Evidence

☐ Teacher makes sure low-expectancy students are asked questions at the same rate as high-expectancy students.

☐ Teacher makes sure low-expectancy students are asked complex questions at the same rate as high-expectancy students.

Student Evidence

☐ When asked, students say the teacher expects everyone to participate.

☐ When asked, students say the teacher asks difficult questions of everyone.

Scale

	Innovating (4)	Applying (3)	Developing (2)	Beginning (1)	Not Using (0)
Asking questions of low-expectancy students	Adapts and creates new strategies for unique student needs and situations	Asks questions of low-expectancy students with the same frequency and depth as with high-expectancy students, and monitors the quality of participation of low-expectancy students	Asks questions of low-expectancy students with the same frequency and depth as with high-expectancy students	Uses strategy incorrectly or with parts missing	Strategy was called for but not exhibited

18. Probing Incorrect Answers with Low-Expectancy Students

The teacher probes incorrect answers of low-expectancy students in the same manner as with high-expectancy students.	*Notes*

Teacher Evidence

☐ Teacher asks low-expectancy students to further explain their answers when they are incorrect.

☐ Teacher rephrases questions for low-expectancy students when they provide an incorrect answer.

☐ Teacher breaks a question into smaller and simpler parts when a low-expectancy student answers a question incorrectly.

☐ When low-expectancy students demonstrate frustration, the teacher allows them to collect their thoughts and goes back to them at a later point.

Student Evidence

☐ When asked, students say that the teacher won't "let you off the hook."

☐ When asked, students say that the teacher "won't give up on you."

☐ When asked, students say the teacher helps them answer questions successfully.

Scale

	Innovating (4)	Applying (3)	Developing (2)	Beginning (1)	Not Using (0)
Probing incorrect answers with low-expectancy students	Adapts and creates new strategies for unique student needs and situations	Probes incorrect answers of low-expectancy students in the same manner as with high-expectancy students, and monitors the level and quality of low-expectancy students' responses	Probes incorrect answers of low-expectancy students in the same manner as with high-expectancy students	Uses strategy incorrectly or with parts missing	Strategy was called for but not exhibited

Observational Protocol (Short Form)

I. Lesson Segments Involving Routine Events							
Design Question 1: What will I do to establish and communicate learning goals, track student progress, and celebrate success?							
1. Providing clear learning goals and scales to measure those goals (e.g., the teacher provides or reminds students about a specific learning goal)	Notes						
		I (4)	A (3)	D (2)	B (1)	NU (0)	
2. Tracking student progress (e.g., using formative assessment, the teacher helps students chart their individual and group progress on a learning goal)	Notes						
		I (4)	A (3)	D (2)	B (1)	NU (0)	
3. Celebrating student success (e.g., the teacher helps students acknowledge and celebrate their current status on a learning goal as well as knowledge gain)	Notes						
		I (4)	A (3)	D (2)	B (1)	NU (0)	
Design Question 6: What will I do to establish and maintain classroom rules and procedures?							
4. Establishing classroom routines (e.g., the teacher reminds students of a rule or procedure or establishes a new rule or procedure)	Notes						
		I (4)	A (3)	D (2)	B (1)	NU (0)	
5. Organizing the physical layout of the classroom for learning (e.g., the teacher organizes materials, traffic patterns, and displays to enhance learning)	Notes						
		I (4)	A (3)	D (2)	B (1)	NU (0)	
II. Lesson Segments Addressing Content							
Design Question 2: What will I do to help students effectively interact with new knowledge?							
1. Identifying critical information (e.g., the teacher provides cues as to which information is important)	Notes						
		I (4)	A (3)	D (2)	B (1)	NU (0)	
2. Organizing students to interact with new knowledge (e.g., the teacher organizes students into dyads or triads to discuss small chunks of content)	Notes						
		I (4)	A (3)	D (2)	B (1)	NU (0)	

	Notes		I (4)	A (3)	D (2)	B (1)	NU (0)
3. Previewing new content (e.g., the teacher uses strategies such as K-W-L, advance organizers, or preview questions)	Notes						
4. Chunking content into "digestible bites" (e.g., the teacher presents content in small portions that are tailored to students' level of understanding)	Notes		I (4)	A (3)	D (2)	B (1)	NU (0)
5. Group processing of new information (e.g., after each chunk of information, the teacher asks students to summarize and clarify what they have experienced)	Notes		I (4)	A (3)	D (2)	B (1)	NU (0)
6. Elaborating on new information (e.g., the teacher asks questions that require students to make and defend inferences)	Notes		I (4)	A (3)	D (2)	B (1)	NU (0)
7. Recording and representing knowledge (e.g., the teacher asks students to summarize, take notes, or use nonlinguistic representations)	Notes		I (4)	A (3)	D (2)	B (1)	NU (0)
8. Reflecting on learning (e.g., the teacher asks students to reflect on what they understand or what they are still confused about)	Notes		I (4)	A (3)	D (2)	B (1)	NU (0)

Design Question 3: What will I do to help students practice and deepen their understanding of new knowledge?

	Notes		I (4)	A (3)	D (2)	B (1)	NU (0)
9. Reviewing content (e.g., the teacher briefly reviews related content addressed previously)	Notes		I (4)	A (3)	D (2)	B (1)	NU (0)
10. Organizing students to practice and deepen knowledge (e.g., the teacher organizes students into groups designed to review information or practice skills)	Notes		I (4)	A (3)	D (2)	B (1)	NU (0)
11. Using homework (e.g., the teacher uses homework for independent practice or to elaborate on information)	Notes		I (4)	A (3)	D (2)	B (1)	NU (0)
12. Examining similarities and differences (e.g., the teacher engages students in comparing, classifying, and creating analogies and metaphors)	Notes		I (4)	A (3)	D (2)	B (1)	NU (0)

13. Examining errors in reasoning (e.g., the teacher asks students to examine informal fallacies, propaganda, and bias)	Notes		I (4)	A (3)	D (2)	B (1)	NU (0)
14. Practicing skills, strategies, and processes (e.g., the teacher uses massed and distributed practice)	Notes		I (4)	A (3)	D (2)	B (1)	NU (0)
15. Revising knowledge (e.g., the teacher asks students to revise entries in notebooks to clarify and add to previous information)	Notes		I (4)	A (3)	D (2)	B (1)	NU (0)

Design Question 4: What will I do to help students generate and test hypotheses about new knowledge?

16. Organizing students for cognitively complex tasks (e.g., the teacher organizes students into small groups to facilitate cognitively complex tasks)	Notes		I (4)	A (3)	D (2)	B (1)	NU (0)
17. Engaging students in cognitively complex tasks involving hypothesis generating and testing (e.g., the teacher engages students in decision-making tasks, problem-solving tasks, experimental inquiry tasks, and investigation tasks)	Notes		I (4)	A (3)	D (2)	B (1)	NU (0)
18. Providing resources and guidance (e.g., the teacher makes resources available that are specific to cognitively complex tasks and helps students execute such tasks)	Notes		I (4)	A (3)	D (2)	B (1)	NU (0)

III. Lesson Segments Enacted on the Spot

Design Question 5: What will I do to engage students?

1. Noticing and reacting when students are not engaged (e.g., the teacher scans the classroom to monitor students' level of engagement)	Notes		I (4)	A (3)	D (2)	B (1)	NU (0)
2. Using academic games (e.g., when students are not engaged, the teacher uses adaptations of popular games to reengage them and focus their attention on academic content)	Notes		I (4)	A (3)	D (2)	B (1)	NU (0)
3. Managing response rates during questioning (e.g., the teacher uses strategies to ensure that multiple students respond to questions such as response cards, response chaining, and voting technologies)	Notes		I (4)	A (3)	D (2)	B (1)	NU (0)

4. Using physical movement (e.g., the teacher uses strategies that require students to move physically, such as voting with your feet and physical reenactments of content)	Notes						
			I (4)	A (3)	D (2)	B (1)	NU (0)
5. Maintaining a lively pace (e.g., the teacher slows and quickens the pace of instruction in such a way as to enhance engagement)	Notes						
			I (4)	A (3)	D (2)	B (1)	NU (0)
6. Demonstrating intensity and enthusiasm (e.g., the teacher uses verbal and nonverbal signals that he or she is enthusiastic about the content)	Notes						
			I (4)	A (3)	D (2)	B (1)	NU (0)
7. Using friendly controversy (e.g., the teacher uses techniques that require students to take and defend a position about content)	Notes						
			I (4)	A (3)	D (2)	B (1)	NU (0)
8. Providing opportunities for students to talk about themselves (e.g., the teacher uses techniques that allow students to relate content to their personal lives and interests)	Notes						
			I (4)	A (3)	D (2)	B (1)	NU (0)
9. Presenting unusual or intriguing information (e.g., the teacher provides or encourages the identification of intriguing information about the content)	Notes						
			I (4)	A (3)	D (2)	B (1)	NU (0)

Design Question 7: What will I do to recognize and acknowledge adherence or lack of adherence to classroom rules and procedures?

10. Demonstrating "withitness" (e.g., the teacher is aware of variations in student behavior that might indicate potential disruptions and attends to them immediately)	Notes						
			I (4)	A (3)	D (2)	B (1)	NU (0)
11. Applying consequences (e.g., the teacher applies consequences for lack of adherence to rules and procedures consistently and fairly)	Notes						
			I (4)	A (3)	D (2)	B (1)	NU (0)
12. Acknowledging adherence to rules and procedures (e.g., the teacher acknowledges adherence to rules and procedures consistently and fairly)	Notes						
			I (4)	A (3)	D (2)	B (1)	NU (0)

Design Question 8: What will I do to establish and maintain effective relationships with students?

13. Understanding students' interests and backgrounds (e.g., the teacher seeks out knowledge about students and uses that knowledge to engage in informal, friendly discussions with students)	Notes						
			I (4)	A (3)	D (2)	B (1)	NU (0)

14. Using behaviors that indicate affection for students (e.g., the teacher uses humor and friendly banter appropriately with students)	Notes						
			I (4)	A (3)	D (2)	B (1)	NU (0)

15. Displaying objectivity and control (e.g., the teacher behaves in ways that indicate he or she does not take infractions personally)	Notes						
			I (4)	A (3)	D (2)	B (1)	NU (0)

Design Question 9: What will I do to communicate high expectations for all students?

16. Demonstrating value and respect for low-expectancy students (e.g., the teacher demonstrates the same positive affective tone with low-expectancy students as with high-expectancy students)	Notes						
			I (4)	A (3)	D (2)	B (1)	NU (0)

17. Asking questions of low-expectancy students (e.g., the teacher asks questions of low-expectancy students with the same frequency and level of difficulty as with high-expectancy students)	Notes						
			I (4)	A (3)	D (2)	B (1)	NU (0)

18. Probing incorrect answers with low-expectancy students (e.g., the teacher inquires into incorrect answers with low-expectancy students with the same depth and rigor as with high-expectancy students)	Notes						
			I (4)	A (3)	D (2)	B (1)	NU (0)

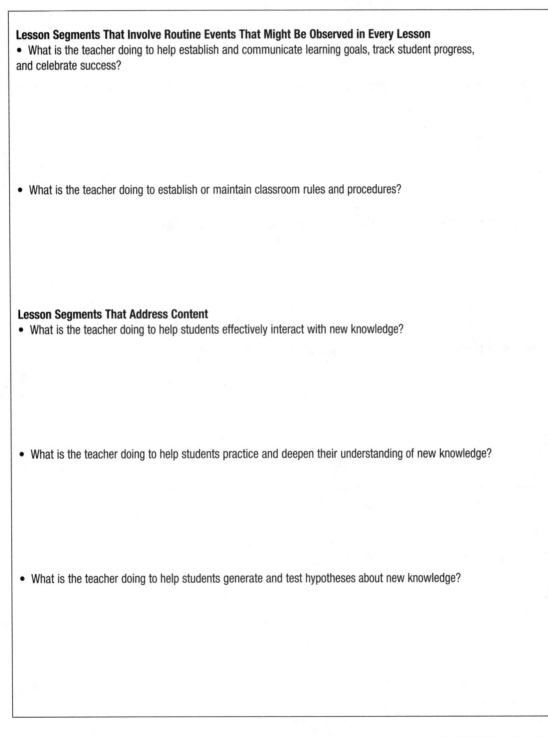

APPENDIX C   Observational Protocol (Snapshot Form)

Lesson Segments That Involve Routine Events That Might Be Observed in Every Lesson
- What is the teacher doing to help establish and communicate learning goals, track student progress, and celebrate success?

- What is the teacher doing to establish or maintain classroom rules and procedures?

Lesson Segments That Address Content
- What is the teacher doing to help students effectively interact with new knowledge?

- What is the teacher doing to help students practice and deepen their understanding of new knowledge?

- What is the teacher doing to help students generate and test hypotheses about new knowledge?

Lesson Segments That Are Enacted on the Spot

• What is the teacher doing to engage students?

• What is the teacher doing to recognize and acknowledge adherence and lack of adherence to classroom rules and procedures?

• What is the teacher doing to establish and maintain effective relationships with students?

• What is the teacher doing to communicate high expectations for all students?

APPENDIX D	Planning and Preparing

PLANNING AND PREPARING FOR LESSONS AND UNITS

---

1. Planning and preparing for effective scaffolding of information within lessons

Innovating (4)	Applying (3)	Developing (2)	Beginning (1)	Not Using (0)
The teacher is a recognized leader in helping others with this activity.	Within lessons, the teacher organizes content in such a way that each new piece of information clearly builds on the previous piece.	The teacher scaffolds the information, but the relationship between elements is not made clear.	The teacher attempts to perform this activity but does not actually complete or follow through with these attempts.	The teacher makes no attempt to perform this activity.

2. Planning and preparing for lessons within a unit that progress toward a deep understanding and transfer of content

Innovating (4)	Applying (3)	Developing (2)	Beginning (1)	Not Using (0)
The teacher is a recognized leader in helping others with this activity.	The teacher organizes lessons within a unit so that students move from an understanding to applying the content through authentic tasks.	The teacher organizes lessons within a unit so that students move from surface to deeper understanding of content, but does not require students to apply the content in authentic ways.	The teacher attempts to perform this activity but does not actually complete or follow through with these attempts.	The teacher makes no attempt to perform this activity.

3. Planning and preparing for appropriate attention to established content standards

Innovating (4)	Applying (3)	Developing (2)	Beginning (1)	Not Using (0)
The teacher is a recognized leader in helping others with this activity.	The teacher ensures that lessons and units include the important content identified by the district and the manner in which that content should be sequenced.	The teacher ensures that lessons and units include the important content identified by the district, but does not address the proper sequencing of content.	The teacher attempts to perform this activity but does not actually complete or follow through with these attempts.	The teacher makes no attempt to perform this activity.

PLANNING AND PREPARING FOR USE OF MATERIALS AND TECHNOLOGY

1. Planning and preparing for the use of available materials for upcoming units and lessons

Innovating (4)	Applying (3)	Developing (2)	Beginning (1)	Not Using (0)
The teacher is a recognized leader in helping others with this activity.	The teacher identifies the available traditional materials that can enhance student understanding and the manner in which they will be used.	The teacher identifies the available traditional materials that can enhance student understanding, but does not identify the manner in which they will be used.	The teacher attempts to perform this activity but does not actually complete or follow through with these attempts.	The teacher makes no attempt to perform this activity.

2. Planning and preparing for the use of available technologies such as interactive whiteboards, response systems, and computers

Innovating (4)	Applying (3)	Developing (2)	Beginning (1)	Not Using (0)
The teacher is a recognized leader in helping others with this activity.	The teacher identifies the available technologies that can enhance student understanding and the manner in which they will be used.	The teacher identifies the available technologies that can enhance student understanding, but does not identify the manner in which they will be used.	The teacher attempts to perform this activity but does not actually complete or follow through with these attempts.	The teacher makes no attempt to perform this activity.

—————————— **PLANNING AND PREPARING FOR SPECIAL NEEDS OF STUDENTS** ——————————

1. Planning and preparing for the needs of English language learners

Innovating (4)	Applying (3)	Developing (2)	Beginning (1)	Not Using (0)
The teacher is a recognized leader in helping others with this activity.	The teacher identifies the needs of English language learners and the adaptations that will be made to meet these needs.	The teacher identifies the needs of English language learners, but does not articulate the adaptations that will be made to meet these needs.	The teacher attempts to perform this activity but does not actually complete or follow through with these attempts.	The teacher makes no attempt to perform this activity.

2. Planning and preparing for the needs of special education students

Innovating (4)	Applying (3)	Developing (2)	Beginning (1)	Not Using (0)
The teacher is a recognized leader in helping others with this activity.	The teacher identifies the needs of special education students and the adaptations that will be made to meet these needs.	The teacher identifies the needs of special education students, but does not articulate the adaptations that will be made to meet these needs.	The teacher attempts to perform this activity but does not actually complete or follow through with these attempts.	The teacher makes no attempt to perform this activity.

3. Planning and preparing for the needs of students who come from home environments that offer little support for schooling

Innovating (4)	Applying (3)	Developing (2)	Beginning (1)	Not Using (0)
The teacher is a recognized leader in helping others with this activity.	The teacher identifies the needs of students who come from home environments that do not support learning and the adaptations that will be made to meet these needs.	The teacher identifies the needs of students who come from home environments that do not support learning, but does not articulate the adaptations that will be made to meet these needs.	The teacher attempts to perform this activity but does not actually complete or follow through with these attempts.	The teacher makes no attempt to perform this activity.

Reflecting on Teaching

EVALUATING PERSONAL PERFORMANCE

1. Identifying specific areas of pedagogical strength and weakness within Domain 1

Innovating (4)	Applying (3)	Developing (2)	Beginning (1)	Not Using (0)
The teacher is a recognized leader in helping others with this activity.	The teacher identifies specific strategies and behaviors on which to improve from routine lesson segments, content lesson segments, and segments that are enacted on the spot.	The teacher identifies specific strategies and behaviors on which to improve, but does not select the strategies and behaviors that are most useful for his or her development.	The teacher attempts to perform this activity but does not actually complete or follow through with these attempts.	The teacher makes no attempt to perform this activity.

2. Evaluating the effectiveness of individual lessons and units

Innovating (4)	Applying (3)	Developing (2)	Beginning (1)	Not Using (0)
The teacher is a recognized leader in helping others with this activity.	The teacher determines how effective a lesson or unit was in terms of enhancing student achievement and identifies causes of success or failure.	The teacher determines how effective a lesson or unit was in terms of enhancing student achievement, but does not accurately identify causes of success or failure.	The teacher attempts to perform this activity but does not actually complete or follow through with these attempts.	The teacher makes no attempt to perform this activity.

3. Evaluating the effectiveness of specific pedagogical strategies and behaviors across different categories of students (i.e., different socioeconomic groups, different ethnic groups)

Innovating (4)	Applying (3)	Developing (2)	Beginning (1)	Not Using (0)
The teacher is a recognized leader in helping others with this activity.	The teacher determines the effectiveness of specific strategies and behaviors regarding the achievement of subgroups of students and identifies the reasons for discrepancies.	The teacher determines the effectiveness of specific strategies and behaviors regarding the achievement of subgroups of students, but does not accurately identify the reasons for discrepancies.	The teacher attempts to perform this activity but does not actually complete or follow through with these attempts.	The teacher makes no attempt to perform this activity.

—————— **DEVELOPING AND IMPLEMENTING A PROFESSIONAL GROWTH AND DEVELOPMENT PLAN** ——————

1. Developing a written growth and development plan

Innovating (4)	Applying (3)	Developing (2)	Beginning (1)	Not Using (0)
The teacher is a recognized leader in helping others with this activity.	The teacher develops a written professional growth and development plan with milestones and time lines.	The teacher develops a written professional growth and development plan, but does not articulate clear milestones and time lines.	The teacher attempts to perform this activity but does not actually complete or follow through with these attempts.	The teacher makes no attempt to perform this activity.

2. Monitoring progress relative to the professional growth and development plan

Innovating (4)	Applying (3)	Developing (2)	Beginning (1)	Not Using (0)
The teacher is a recognized leader in helping others with this activity.	The teacher charts his or her progress on the professional growth and development plan using established milestones and timelines and makes adaptations as needed.	The teacher charts his or her progress on the professional growth and development plan using established milestones and time lines, but does not make adaptations as needed.	The teacher attempts to perform this activity but does not actually complete or follow through with these attempts.	The teacher makes no attempt to perform this activity.

APPENDIX F   Collegiality and Professionalism

PROMOTING A POSITIVE ENVIRONMENT

1. Promoting positive interactions about colleagues

Innovating (4)	Applying (3)	Developing (2)	Beginning (1)	Not Using (0)
The teacher is a recognized leader in helping others with this activity.	The teacher interacts with other teachers in a positive manner and helps extinguish negative conversations about other teachers.	The teacher interacts with other teachers in a positive manner, but does not help extinguish negative conversations about other teachers.	The teacher attempts to perform this activity but does not actually complete or follow through with these attempts.	The teacher makes no attempt to perform this activity.

2. Promoting positive interactions about students and parents

Innovating (4)	Applying (3)	Developing (2)	Beginning (1)	Not Using (0)
The teacher is a recognized leader in helping others with this activity.	The teacher interacts with students and parents in a positive manner and helps extinguish negative conversations about students and parents.	The teacher interacts with students and parents in a positive manner, but does not help extinguish negative conversations about students and parents.	The teacher attempts to perform this activity but does not actually complete or follow through with these attempts.	The teacher makes no attempt to perform this activity.

————————————— **PROMOTING EXCHANGE OF IDEAS AND STRATEGIES** —————————————

1. Seeking mentorship for areas of need or interest

Innovating (4)	Applying (3)	Developing (2)	Beginning (1)	Not Using (0)
The teacher is a recognized leader in helping others with this activity.	The teacher seeks help and mentorship from colleagues regarding specific classroom strategies and behaviors.	The teacher seeks help and mentorship from colleagues, but not at a specific enough level to enhance his or her pedagogical skill.	The teacher attempts to perform this activity but does not actually complete or follow through with these attempts.	The teacher makes no attempt to perform this activity.

2. Mentoring other teachers and sharing ideas and strategies

Innovating (4)	Applying (3)	Developing (2)	Beginning (1)	Not Using (0)
The teacher is a recognized leader in helping others with this activity.	The teacher provides other teachers with help and input regarding classroom strategies and behaviors.	The teacher provides other teachers with help and input regarding classroom strategies and behaviors, but not at a specific enough level to enhance their pedagogical skill.	The teacher attempts to perform this activity but does not actually complete or follow through with these attempts.	The teacher makes no attempt to perform this activity.

————————————— **PROMOTING DISTRICT AND SCHOOL DEVELOPMENT** —————————————

1. Adhering to district and school rules and procedures

Innovating (4)	Applying (3)	Developing (2)	Beginning (1)	Not Using (0)
The teacher is a recognized leader in helping others with this activity.	The teacher is aware of district and school rules and procedures and adheres to them.	The teacher is aware of district and school rules and procedures but does not adhere, to all of these rules and procedures.	The teacher attempts to perform this activity but does not actually complete or follow through with these attempts.	The teacher makes no attempt to perform this activity.

2. Participating in district and school initiatives

Innovating (4)	Applying (3)	Developing (2)	Beginning (1)	Not Using (0)
The teacher is a recognized leader in helping others with this activity.	The teacher is aware of the district's and school's initiatives and participates in them in accordance with his or her talents and availability.	The teacher is aware of the district's and school's initiatives, but does not participate in them in accordance with his or her talents and availability.	The teacher attempts to perform this activity but does not actually complete or follow through with these attempts.	The teacher makes no attempt to perform this activity.

References

Alvermann, D. E., & Boothby, P. R. (1986). Children's transfer of graphic organizer instruction. *Reading Psychology, 7*(2), 87–100.

Ambady, N., & Rosenthal, R. (1992). Thin slices of expressive behavior as predictors of interpersonal consequences: A meta-analysis. *Psychological Bulletin, 111*(2), 256–274.

Ambady, N., & Rosenthal, R. (1993). Half a minute: Predicting teacher evaluations from thin slices of nonverbal behavior and physical attractiveness. *Journal of Personality and Social Psychology, 64*(3), 431–441.

Anderson, L., Evertson, C., & Emmer, E. (1980). Dimensions in classroom management derived from recent research. *Journal of Curriculum Studies, 12,* 343–356.

Anderson, V., & Hidi, S. (1988/1989). Teaching students to summarize. *Educational Leadership, 46,* 26–28.

Aubusson, P., Foswill, S., Barr, R., & Perkovic, L. (1997). What happens when students do simulation-role-play in science. *Research in Science Education, 27*(4), 565–579.

Ausubel, D. P. (1968). *Educational psychology: A cognitive view.* New York: Holt, Rinehart & Winston.

Bangert-Drowns, R. L., Kulik, C. C., Kulik, J. A., & Morgan, M. (1991). The instructional effects of feedback in test-like events. *Review of Educational Research, 61*(2), 213–238.

Barton, P. E. (2006). Needed: Higher standards for accountability. *Educational Leadership, 64*(3), 28–31.

Berliner, D. (1982). On improving teacher effectiveness: A conversation with David Berliner. *Educational Leadership, 40*(1), 12–15.

Berliner, D. C. (1986). In pursuit of the expert pedagogue. *Educational Researcher, 15*(7), 5–13.

Bloom, B. S. (1976). *Human characteristics and school learning.* New York: McGraw-Hill.

Blumberg, A. (1985). Where we came from: Notes on supervision in the 1840's. *Journal of Curriculum and Supervision, 1*(1), 56–65.

Blumenfeld, P. C., & Meece, J. L. (1988). Task factors, teacher behavior, and students' involvement and use of learning strategies in science. *Elementary School Journal, 88*(3), 235–250.

Bolton, D. L. (1973). *Selection and evaluation of teachers.* Berkeley, CA: McCutchen.

Brekelmans, M., Wubbels, T., & Creton, H. A. (1990). A study of student perceptions of physics teacher behavior. *Journal of Research in Science Teaching, 27,* 335, 350.

Brophy, J. E., & Evertson, C. M. (1976). *Learning from teaching: A developmental perspective.* Boston: Allyn & Bacon.

Bruce, R. F., & Hoehn, L. (1980, December). *Supervisory practice in Georgia and Ohio.* Paper presented at the Annual Meeting of the Council of Professors of Instructional Supervision, Hollywood, FL.

Burke, P., & Krey, R. (2005). *Supervision: A guide to instructional leadership* (2nd ed.). Springfield, IL: Thomas.

Calandra, B., Brantley-Dias, L., Lee, J. K., & Fox, D. L. (2009, Fall). Using video editing to cultivate novice teachers' practice. *Journal of Research on Technology in Education, 42*(1), 73–94.

Charalambos, V., Michalinos, Z., & Chamberlain, R. (2004). The design of online learning communities: Critical issues. *Educational Media International,* 135–143.

City, E. A., Elmore, R. F., Fiarman, S. E., & Teitel, L. (2009). *Instructional rounds in education: A network approach to improving teaching and learning.* Cambridge, MA: Harvard University Press.

Clark, C., & Peterson, P. (1986). Teacher's thought processes. In M. C. Wittrock (Ed.), *Handbook of research on teaching* (3rd ed., pp. 255–296). New York: Macmillan.

Cochran-Smith, M., & Power, C. (2010). New direction in teacher preparation. *Educational Leadership, 67*(8) 6–13.

Cogan, M. (1973). *Clinical supervision.* Boston: Houghton Mifflin.

Coggshall, J. G., Ott, A., & Lasagna, M. (2010). *Convergence and contradictions in teachers' perceptions of policy reform ideas.* Retaining Teacher Talent, Report No. 3. Naperville, IL: Learning Point Associates and New York: Public Agenda. Available: www.learningpt.org/expertise/educatorquality/genY/CommunicatingReform/index.php

Coleman, E. (1945). The "supervisory visit." *Educational Leadership, 2*(4), 164–167.

Connell, J. P., Spencer, M. B., & Aber, J. L. (1994). Educational risk and resilience in African-American youth: Context, self, action, and outcomes in school. *Child Development, 65,* 493–506.

Connell, J. P., & Wellborn, J. G. (1991). Competence, autonomy, and relatedness: A motivational analysis of self-system processes. In M. Gunnar & L. A. Sroufe (Eds.), *Minnesota symposium on child psychology* (Vol. 23, pp. 21–56). Chicago: University of Chicago Press.

Cooper, H., Robinson, J. C., & Patall, E. A. (2006). Does homework improve academic achievement? A synthesis of research, 1987–2003. *Review of Educational Research, 76*(1), 1–62.

Cross, K. P. (1998). Classroom research: Implementing the scholarship of teaching. In T. Angelo (Ed.), *Classroom assessment and research: An update on uses, approaches, and research findings* (pp. 5–12). San Francisco: Jossey-Bass.

Cubberley, E. P. (1929). *Public school administration* (3rd ed.). Boston: Houghton Mifflin.

Danielson, C. (1996). *Enhancing professional practice: A framework for teaching.* Alexandria, VA: Association for Supervision and Curriculum Development.

Danielson, C. (2007). *Enhancing professional practice: A framework for teaching* (2nd ed.). Alexandria, VA: Association for Supervision and Curriculum Development.

Darling-Hammond, L. (2009). Teaching and the change wars: The professional hypothesis. In A. Hargreaves & M. Fullan (Eds.), *Change wars* (pp. 45–70). Bloomington, IN: Solution Tree.

David, J. L. (2010). What research says about using value-added measures to evaluate teachers. *Educational Leadership, 67*(8), 81–83.

Deci, E. L., Ryan, R. M., & Koestner, R. (2001). The pervasive effects of rewards on intrinsic motivation: Response to Cameron (2001). *Review of Educational Research, 71*(1), 43–51.

Dewey, J. (1938). *Experience and education.* New York: Macmillan.

Dewey, J. (1981). *The philosophy of John Dewey* (J. McDermott, Ed.). Chicago: University of Chicago Press.

Downey, C. J., & Frase, L. E. (2001). *Participant's manual for conducting walk-through with reflective feedback to maximize student achievement* (2nd ed.). Huxley, IA: Curriculum Management Services.

Downey, C. J., & Frase L. E. (2004). *Participant's manual for conducting walk-through with reflective feedback to maximize student achievement* (2nd ed.). Huxley, IA: Curriculum Management Services.

Downey, C. J., Steffy, B. E., English, F. W., Frase, L. E., & Poston, W. K., Jr. (2004). *The three-minute classroom walk-through: Changing school supervisory practice one teacher at a time.* Thousand Oaks, CA: Corwin Press.

Doyle, W. (1983). Academic work. *Review of Educational Research, 53*(2), 159–199.

Doyle, W. (1986). Classroom organization and management. In M. C. Wittrock (Ed.), *Handbook of research on teaching* (3rd ed., pp. 392–431). New York: Macmillan.

Druyan, S. (1997). Effects of the kinesthetic conflict on promoting scientific reasoning. *Journal of Research in Science Teaching, 34*(10), 1083–1099.

DuFour, R., DuFour, R., & Eaker, R. (2008). *Revisiting professional learning communities at work.* Bloomington, IN: Solution Tree.

DuFour, R., DuFour, R., Eaker, R., & Karhanek, G. (2004). *Whatever it takes: How professional learning communities respond when kids don't learn.* Bloomington, IN: National Educational Service.

DuFour, R., & Eaker, R. (1998). *Professional learning communities at work: Best practices for enhancing student achievement.* Bloomington, IN: National Educational Service.

DuFour, R., Eaker, R., & DuFour, R. (2005). *On common ground: The power of professional learning communities.* Bloomington, IN: Solution Tree.

Editorial Projects in Education. (2009). *The Obama education plan: An Education Week guide.* San Francisco: Jossey-Bass.

Eisenhart, M. (1977, May). *Maintaining control: Teacher competence in the classroom.* Paper presented at the American Anthropological Association, Houston, TX.

Emmer, E. T., Evertson, C., & Anderson, L. (1980). Effective classroom management at the beginning of the school year. *Elementary School Journal, 80*(5), 219–231.

Ericsson, A., Charness, N., Feltovich, P., & Hoffman, R. (Eds.). (2006). *The Cambridge handbook of expertise and expert performance.* New York: Cambridge University Press.

Ericsson, K. A., & Charness, N. (1994). Expert performance: Its structure and acquisition. *American Psychologist, 49*(8), 725–747.

Ericsson, K. A., Krampe, R. T., & Tesch-Romer, C. (1993). The role of deliberate practice in the acquisition of expert performance. *Psychological Review, 100*(3), 363–406.

Estes Park News. (2010, January 25). *Estes Park teacher Jeff Arnold renews National Certificate of Teaching Excellence.* Retrieved from www.estesparknews.com/?p=4048

Evertson, C., & Weinstein, C. S. (Eds.). (2006). *Handbook of classroom management: Research, practice, and contemporary issues.* Mahwah, NJ: Erlbaum.

Fehr, S. (2001, August). *The role of educational supervision in the United States public schools from 1970 to 2000 as reflected in the supervision literature.* Unpublished doctoral dissertation, Pennsylvania State University, State College.

Flinders, D. J. (1988). Teacher isolation and the new reform. *Journal of Curriculum and Supervision, 4*(1), 17–29.

Friedkin, N. E., & Slater, M. R. (1994). School leadership and performance: A social network approach. *Sociology of Education, 67,* 139–157.

Garmston, R. J., & Wellman, B. M. (1999). *The adaptive school: A sourcebook for developing collaborative groups.* Norwood, MA: Christopher-Gordon.

Gawande, A. (2009, June 1). The cost conundrum: What a Texas town can teach us about health care. *The New Yorker,* 36–44.

Gijbels, D., Dochy, F., Van den Bossche, P., & Segers, M. (2005). Effects of problem-based learning: A meta-analysis from the angle of assessment. *Review of Educational Research, 75*(1), 27–61.

Glatthorn, A. (1984). *Differentiated supervision.* Alexandria, VA: Association for Supervision and Curriculum Development.

Glickman, C. D. (1985). *Supervision of instruction: A developmental approach.* Boston: Allyn & Bacon.

Glickman, C., Gordon, S., & Ross-Gordon, J. (1998). *Supervision of instruction: A developmental approach* (4th ed.). Boston: Allyn & Bacon.

Goldhammer, R. (1969). *Clinical supervision: Special methods for the supervision of teachers.* New York: Holt, Rinehart & Winston.

Goldhammer, R., Anderson, R., & Krajewski, R. (1993). *Clinical supervision: Special methods for the supervision of teachers.* Orlando, FL: Harcourt Brace College Publishers.

Good, T. L., & Brophy, J. E. (2003). *Looking in classrooms* (9th ed.). Boston: Allyn & Bacon.

Good, T. L., Grouws, D. A., & Ebmeier, H. (1983). *Active mathematics teaching.* Research on Teaching monograph series. New York: Longman.

Goodlad, J. I. (1984). *A place called school: Prospects for the future.* New York: McGraw-Hill.

Grossman, P., & Loeb, S. (2010). Learning from multiple routes. *Educational Leadership, 67*(8), 22–27.

Haas, M. (2005). Teaching methods for secondary algebra: A meta-analysis of findings. *NASSP Bulletin, 89*(642), 24–46.

Halpern, D. F. (1984). *Thought and knowledge: An introduction to critical thinking.* Hillsdale, NJ: Erlbaum.

Halpern, D. F., Hansen, C., & Reifer, D. (1990). Analogies as an aid to understanding and memory. *Journal of Educational Psychology, 82*(2), 298–305.

Hattie, J. (1992). Measuring the effects of schooling. *Australian Journal of Education, 36*(1), 5–13.

Hattie, J. (2009). *Visible learning: A synthesis of over 800 meta-analyses relating to achievement.* New York: Routledge.

Hattie, J., Biggs, J., & Purdie, N. (1996). Effects of learning skills interventions on student learning: A meta-analysis. *Review of Educational Research, 66*(2), 99–136.

Hattie, J., & Timperley, H. (2007). The power of feedback. *Review of Educational Research, 77*(1), 81–112.

Hidi, S., & Anderson, V. (1987). Providing written summaries: Task demands, cognitive operations, and implications for instruction. *Reviewing Educational Research, 56,* 473–493.

Hillocks, G. (1986). *Research on written composition.* Urbana, IL: ERIC Clearinghouse on Reading and Communication Skills and National Conference on Research in English.

Hunter, M. (1980, February). Six types of supervisory conferences. *Educational Leadership, 37*(5), 408–412.

Hunter, M. (1984). Knowing, teaching, and supervising. In P. Hosford (Ed.), *Using what we know about teaching* (pp. 169–192). Alexandria, VA: Association for Supervision and Curriculum Development.

Iwanicki, E. F. (1981). Contract plans. In J. Millman (Ed.), *Handbook of teacher evaluation.* Beverly Hills, CA: Sage.

Jackson, C. K., & Bruegmann, E. (2009). *Teaching students and teaching each other: The importance of peer learning for teachers.* NBER Working Paper Series. Cambridge, MA: National Bureau of Economic Research.

Jaffe, R., Moir, E., Swanson, E., & Wheeler, G. (2006). E-mentoring for student success: Online mentoring and professional development for new science teachers. In C. Dede (Ed.), *Online professional development for teachers: Emerging models and methods* (pp. 89–116). Cambridge, MA: Harvard Education Press.

Johnson, S. M., & Papay, J. P. (2010). Merit pay for a new generation. *Educational Leadership, 67*(8), 48–53.

Joyce, B., & Showers, B. (1982). The coaching of teaching. *Educational Leadership, 40*(1), 4–10.

King, S. E. (2008, Winter). Inspiring critical reflection in preservice teachers. *Physical Educator, 65*(1), 21–29.

Kleinman, G. M. (2001). *Meeting the need for high quality teachers: E-learning solutions.* White paper distributed at the U.S. Department of Education Secretary's No Child Left Behind Leadership Summit, Newton, MA. Newton, MA: Education Development Center.

Knowles, M. (1980). My farewell address . . . Andragogy no panacea, no ideology. *Training and Development, 34*(18), 48–50.

Kumar, D. D. (1991). A meta-analysis of the relationship between science instruction and student engagement. *Education Review, 43*(1), 49–66.

Learning Sciences International (2009). Online library of professional development resources. York, PA: Author.

Leinhardt, G. (1990). Capturing craft knowledge in teaching. *Educational Researcher, 19*(2), 18–25.

Leinhardt, G., & Greeno, J. (1986). The cognitive skill of teaching. *Journal of Educational Psychology, 78*(2), 75–95.

Levine, D. U., & Lezotte, L. W. (1990). *Unusually effective schools: A review and analysis of research and practice.* Madison, WI: National Center for Effective Schools Research and Development.

Levinson, D. J. (1977). *The seasons of a man's life.* New York: Knopf.

Lewis, H., & Leps, J. M. (1946). When principals supervise. *Educational Leadership, 3*(4), 160–163.

Lieberman, A., & Rosenholtz, S. (1987). The road to school improvement: Barriers and bridges. In J. Goodlad (Ed.), *The ecology of school renewal: Eighty-sixth yearbook of the National Society for the Study of Education* (pp. 79–98). Chicago: National Society for the Study of Education.

Linden, D. E., Bittner, R. A., Muckli, L., Waltz, J. A., Kriegekorte, N., Goebel, R., Singer, W., & Munk, M. H. (2003). Cortical capacity constraints for visual working memory: Dissociation of FMRI load effects in a fronto-parietal network. *Neuroimage, 20*(3), 1518–1530.

Lipsey, M. W., & Wilson, D. B. (1993). The efficacy of psychological, educational, and behavioral treatment. *American Psychologist, 48*(12), 1181–1209.

Louis, K. S., Kruse, S. D., & Associates. (1995). *Professionalism and community: Perspectives on reforming urban schools.* Thousand Oaks, CA: Corwin Press.

Mahaffey, D., Lind, K., & Derse, L. (2005). *Professional development plan: Educator toolkit.* Milwaukee: Wisconsin Department of Public Instruction.

Marzano, R. J. (1992). *A different kind of classroom: Teaching with dimensions of learning.* Alexandria, VA: Association for Supervision and Curriculum Development.

Marzano, R. J. (2003). *What works in schools: Translating research into action.* Alexandria, VA: Association for Supervision and Curriculum Development.

Marzano, R. J. (2006). *Classroom assessment and grading that work.* Alexandria, VA: Association for Supervision and Curriculum Development.

Marzano, R. J. (2007). *The art and science of teaching: A comprehensive framework for effective instruction.* Alexandria, VA: Association for Supervision and Curriculum Development.

Marzano, R. J. (2009). Setting the record straight on "high yield" strategies. *Phi Delta Kappan, 91*(1), 30–37.

Marzano, R. J. (2010a). Developing expert teachers. In R. J. Marzano (Ed.), *On excellence in teaching* (pp. 213–246). Bloomington, IN: Solution Tree Press.

Marzano, R. J. (2010b). *Formative assessment and standards-based grading.* Bloomington, IN: Marzano Research Laboratory.

Marzano, R. J., & Brown, J. L. (2009). *A handbook for the Art and Science of Teaching.* Alexandria, VA: Association for Supervision and Curriculum Development.

Marzano, R. J., & Kendall, J. S. (2007). *The new taxonomy of educational objectives.* Thousand Oaks, CA: Corwin Press.

Marzano, R. J., Pickering, D. J., & Marzano, J. S. (2003). *Classroom management that works: Research-based strategies for every teacher.* Alexandria, VA: Association for Supervision and Curriculum Development.

Marzano, R. J., Pickering, J. J., & Pollack, J. E. (2001). *Classroom instruction that works: Research-based strategies for increasing student achievement.* Alexandria, VA: Association for Supervision and Curriculum Development.

Marzano, R. J., & Waters, T. (2009). *District leadership that works: Striking the right balance.* Bloomington, IN: Solution Tree Press.

Marzano, R. J., Waters, T., & McNulty, B. A. (2005). *School leadership that works: From research to results.* Alexandria, VA: Association for Supervision and Curriculum Development.

Mayer, R. E. (1989). Models of understanding. *Review of Educational Research, 59*, 43–64.

Mayer, R. E. (2003). *Learning and instruction.* Upper Saddle River, NJ: Merrill/Prentice Hall.

McDaniel, M. A., & Donnelly, C. M. (1996). Learning with analogy and elaborative interrogation. *Journal of Educational Psychology, 88*(3), 508–519.

McGreal, T. (1983). *Successful teacher evaluation.* Alexandria, VA: Association for Supervision and Curriculum Development.

Melchoir, W. (1950). *Instructional supervision: A guide to modern practice.* Boston: Heath.

Moskowitz, G., & Hayman, J. L. (1976). Success strategies of inner-city teachers: A year-long study. *Journal of Educational Research, 69*, 283–289.

Murray, P. (1989). Poetic genius and its classic origins. In P. Murray (Ed), *Genius: The history of the idea* (pp. 9–31). Oxford: Blackwell.

National Board for Professional Teaching Standards. Available: www.nbpts.org

Newby, T. J., Stepich, D. A., Lehman, J. D., Russell, J. D., & Ottenbreit-Leftwich, A. (2011). *Educational technology for teaching and learning* (4th ed.). Boston: Pearson.

Newton, D. P. (1995). Pictorial support for discourse comprehension. *British Journal of Educational Psychology, 64*(2), 221–229.

No Child Left Behind Act of 2001, Pub. L. No. 107-110, 115 Stat. 1425. (2002).

Nuthall, G. (1999). The way students learn: Acquiring knowledge from an integrated science and social studies unit. *Elementary School Journal, 99*(4), 303–341.

Nuthall, G., & Alton-Lee, A. (1995). Assessing classroom learning: How students use their knowledge and experience to answer classroom achievement test questions in science and social studies. *American Educational Research Journal, 32*(1), 185–223.

Patterson, K., Grenny, J., Maxfield, D., McMillan, R., & Switzler, A. (2008). *Influencer: The power to change anything.* New York: McGraw-Hill.

Pressley, M., Wood, E., Woloshyn, V., Martin, V., King, A., & Menke, D. (1992). Encouraging mindful use of prior knowledge: Attempting to construct explanatory answers facilitates learning. *Educational Psychologist, 27,* 91–109.

Reder, L. M. (1980). The role of elaboration in the comprehension and retention of prose: A critical review. *Review of Educational Research, 50*(1), 5–53.

Redfield, D. L., & Rousseau, E. W. (1981). A meta-analysis of experimental research on teacher questioning behavior. *Review of Educational Research, 51*(2), 237–245.

Reeve, J. (2006). Extrinsic rewards and inner motivation. In C. Evertson, C. M. Weinstein, & C. S. Weinstein (Eds.), *Handbook of classroom management: Research, practice, and contemporary issues* (pp. 645–664). Mahwah, NJ: Erlbaum.

Reeves, D. B. (2008). *Reframing teacher leadership to improve your school.* Alexandria, VA: Association for Supervision and Curriculum Development.

Rosaen, C. L., Lundeberg, M., Cooper, M., Fritzen, A., & Terpstra, M. (2008, September/October). Noticing noticing: How does investigation of video records change how teachers reflect on their experiences? *Journal of Teacher Education, 59*(4), 347–360.

Rosenshine, B. (2002). Converging findings on classroom instruction. In A. Molnar (Ed.), *School reform proposals: The research evidence.* Tempe: Arizona State University Research Policy Unit. Retrieved June 2006 from http://epsl.asu.edu/epru/documents/EPRU%202002-101/Chapter%2009-Rosenshine-Final.rtf

Rosenthal, R., & Jacobson, L. (1968). *Pygmalion in the classroom.* New York: Holt, Rinehart & Winston.

Ross, J., & Bruce, C. (2007). Teacher self-assessment: A mechanism for facilitating professional growth. *Teaching & Teacher Education, 23*(2), 146–159. doi:10.1016/j.tate.2006.04.035

Ross, J. A. (1988). Controlling variables: A meta-analysis of training studies. *Review of Educational Research, 58*(4), 405–437.

Rovee-Collier, C. (1995). Time windows in cognitive development. *Developmental Psychology, 31*(2), 147–169.

Sadoski, M., & Paivio, A. (2001). *Imagery and text: A dual coding theory of reading and writing.* Mahwah, NJ: Erlbaum.

Sagor, R. (1992). *How to conduct collaborative action research.* Alexandria, VA: Association for Supervision and Curriculum Development.

Sammons, P. (1999). *School effectiveness: Coming of age in the twenty-first century.* Lisse, The Netherlands: Swets & Zeitlinger.

Sarason, S. B. (1996). *Revisiting "The culture of the school and the problem of change."* New York: Teachers College Press.

Sawchuk, S. (2009, April 1). TAP: More than performance pay. *Education Week.*

Sawchuk, S. (2010, February 10). States rethink policies on National Board teachers. *Education Week,* 1, 13.

Scheerens, J., & Bosker, R. (1997). *The foundations of educational effectiveness.* New York: Elsevier.

Schoenfeld, A. H. (1998). Toward a theory of teaching-in-context. *Issues in Education, 4*(1), 1–94.

Schoenfeld, A. H. (2006). Mathematics teaching and learning. In P. Alexander & P. Winne (Eds.), *Handbook of educational psychology* (2nd ed., pp. 479–510). Mahwah, NJ: Erlbaum.

Schunk, D. H., & Cox, P. D. (1986). Strategy training and attributional feedback with learning disabled students. *Journal of Educational Psychology, 73*(3), 201–209.

Semadeni, J. (2010). When teachers drive their learning. *Educational Leadership, 67*(8), 66–69.

Sewall, M. (2009, Fall). Transforming supervision: Using video elicitation to support preservice teacher-directed reflective conversations. *Issues in Teacher Education, 18*(2), 11–30.

Showers, B., & Joyce, B. (1996). The evolution of peer coaching. *Educational Leadership, 53*(6), 12–16.

Simon, H. A., & Chase, W. G. (1973). Skill in chess. *American Scientist, 61,* 394–403.

Stodolsky, S. (1983). *Classroom activity structures in the fifth grade.* Final report, NIE contract No. 400-77-0094. Chicago: University of Chicago. (ERIC Document Reproduction Service No. ED 242412).

Surowiecki, J. (2004). *The wisdom of crowds: Why the many are smarter than the few and how collective wisdom shapes business, economics, societies, and nations.* New York: Doubleday.

Swearingen, M. (1946, January). Looking at supervision. *Educational Leadership, 3*(4), 146–151.

Taylor, F. W. (1911). *The principles of scientific management.* Reprinted 2007, Sioux Falls, SD: NuVision.

Thirunarayanan, M. O. (2004, February 10). National Board Certification for Teachers: A billion dollar hoax. *Teachers College Record.* Retrieved May 18, 2010, from www.tcrecord.org, ID number 11266.

Thompson, E. (1952). So begins–so ends the supervisor's day. *Educational Leadership, 10*(2), 80–84.

Toch, T., & Rothman, R. (January, 2008). *Rush to judgment: Teacher evaluation in public education.* Washington, DC: Education Sector.

Tracy, S. (1995, May/June). How historical concepts of supervision relate to supervisory practices today. *The Clearing House, 68*(5), 320–324.

Tucker, P. D., & Stronge, J. H. (2005). *Linking teacher evaluation and student learning.* Alexandria, VA: Association for Supervision and Curriculum Development.

Twadell, E. (2008). Win-win contract negotiation: Collective bargaining for student learning. In *The collaborative administrator: Working together as a professional learning community* (pp. 218–233). Bloomington, IN: Solution Tree Press.

U.S. Department of Education. (2002). *Meeting the highly qualified teachers challenge: The secretary's annual report on teacher quality.* Washington, DC: U.S. Department of Education, Office of Postsecondary Education.

Viadero, D., & Honawar, V. (2008, June 18). Credential of NBPTS has impact: Still evidence scant that program transformed field. *Education Week, 1,* 16.

Walberg, H. J. (1999). Productive teaching. In H. C. Waxman & H. J. Walberg (Eds.), *New directions for teaching practice research,* 75–104. Berkeley, CA: McCutchen.

Wang, M. C., Haertel, G. D., & Walberg, H. J. (1993). Toward a knowledge base for school learning. *Review of Educational Research, 63*(3), 249–294.

Weinstein, R. S. (2002). *Reaching higher: The power of expectations in schooling.* Cambridge, MA: Harvard University Press.

Weisberg, D., Sexton, S., Mulhern, J., & Keeling, D. (2009). *The widget effect: Our national failure to acknowledge and act on differences in teacher effectiveness.* Brooklyn, NY: New Teacher Project. Retrieved August 27, 2009, from http://widgeteffect.org/downloads/The Widget Effect.pdf

Welch, M. (1997, April). *Students' use of three-dimensional modeling while designing and making a solution to a technical problem.* Paper presented at the annual meeting of the American Educational Research Association, Chicago.

West, L. H. T., & Fensham, P. J. (1976). Prior knowledge or advance organizers as affective variables in chemical learning. *Journal of Research in Science Teaching, 13,* 297–306.

Wetzel, W. (1929, February). Scientific supervision and curriculum building. *The School Review, 37*(2), 179–192.

Whitehead, M. (1952). Teachers look at supervision. *Educational Leadership, 10*(2), 1011–1106.

Wilkinson, S. S. (1981). The relationship between teacher praise and student achievement: A meta-analysis of selected research. *Dissertation Abstracts International, 41,* 3998A.

Wise, E., Darling-Hammond, L., McLaughlin, M., & Bernstein, H. (1984). *Teacher evaluation: A study of effective practices.* Santa Monica, CA: RAND.

Wise, K. C., & Okey, J. R. (1983). A meta-analysis of the effects of various science teaching strategies on achievement. *Journal of Research in Science Teaching, 20*(5), 415–425.

Wubbles, T., Brekelmans, M., den Brok, P., & van Tartwijk, J. (2006). An interpersonal perspective on classroom management in secondary classrooms in the Netherlands. In C. Evertson & C. S. Weinstein (Eds.), *Handbook of classroom management: Research, practice, and contemporary issues* (pp. 1161–1191). Mahwah, NJ: Erlbaum.

York-Barr, J., & Duke, K. (2004). What do we know about teacher leadership? Findings from two decades of scholarship. *Review of Educational Research, 74*(3), 255–316.

Index

The letter *f* following a page number denotes a figure.

About the Authors

Robert J. Marzano is cofounder and CEO of Marzano Research Laboratory in Englewood, Colorado. A leading researcher in education, he is a speaker, trainer, and author of more than 30 books and 150 articles on topics such as instruction, assessment, writing and implementing standards, cognition, effective leadership, and school intervention. His books include *Designing & Teaching Learning Goals & Objectives, District Leadership That Works, Formative Assessment & Standards-Based Grading, On Excellence in Teaching,* and *The Art and Science of Teaching.* His practical translations of the most current research and theory into classroom strategies are internationally known and widely practiced by both teachers and administrators.

Dr. Marzano received a bachelor's degree from Iona College in New York, a master's degree from Seattle University, and a doctorate from the University of Washington.

Tony Frontier is an assistant professor of doctoral leadership studies and director of teacher education at Cardinal Stritch University in Milwaukee, Wisconsin, where he teaches courses in curriculum development, organizational learning, research methods, and statistics. He began his career in education in 1994 teaching at Roosevelt Middle School of the Arts in Milwaukee Public Schools. He served two years as associate principal at Whitefish Bay High School in Whitefish Bay, Wisconsin, and served nine years as the director of curriculum and instruction for the School District of Whitefish Bay. He has been recognized by Marquette University as the Outstanding Young Alumnus for the School of Education, received the Jack Keane Outstanding Young Educator Award for the State of Wisconsin, was selected as an ASCD Emerging Leader, and has served as President of Wisconsin ASCD. He received a bachelor's degree with majors in sociology and mass communications from the University of Wisconsin, Milwaukee, postbaccalaureate teacher certification from Marquette University, and a master's degree in educational leadership and a PhD in leadership for the advancement of learning and service from Cardinal Stritch University. You can contact him at acfrontier@stritch.edu.

David Livingston is an associate with Marzano Research Laboratory in Englewood, Colorado, specializing in school- and district-level leadership and school improvement. He began his career in education in 1968 with the Chicago Teacher Corps. After a decade of teaching, he served for 20 years as principal of four elementary schools in Oregon and Colorado. From 1998 to 2005, he was executive director of elementary education for the Cherry Creek Schools in Greenwood Village, Colorado. Prior to joining Marzano Research Laboratory, he was principal consultant with Mid-continent Research for Education and Learning in Denver, Colorado. He also serves as facilitator for the Western States Benchmarking Consortium, a network of seven high-performing districts west of the Mississippi River. He received a bachelor's degree in literature from Wheaton College in Illinois, a master's degree in urban education from Roosevelt University in Illinois, and a doctorate in foundations of education from the University of Colorado at Boulder.

Related ASCD Resources: Supervision

At the time of publication, the following ASCD resources were available (ASCD stock numbers appear in parentheses). For up-to-date information about ASCD resources, go to www.ascd.org.

ASCD EDge Group

Exchange ideas and connect with other educators interested in teacher supervision on the social networking site ASCD EDge™ at http://ascdedge.ascd.org/

Print Products

Accountability for Learning: How Teachers and School Leaders Can Take Charge Douglas B. Reeves (#104004)

The Art and Science of Teaching: A Comprehensive Framework for Effective Instruction Robert J. Marzano (#107001)

The Art of School Leadership Thomas R. Hoerr (#105037)

Becoming a Better Teacher: Eight Innovations That Work Giselle O. Martin-Kniep (#100043)

Classroom Management That Works: Research-Based Strategies for Every Teacher Robert J. Marzano, Jana S. Marzano, and Debra J. Pickering (#103027)

Enhancing Professional Practice: A Framework for Teaching, 2nd edition Charlotte Danielson (#106034)

Enhancing Student Achievement: A Framework for School Improvement by Charlotte Danielson (#102109)

Finding Your Leadership Style: A Guide for Educators Jeffrey Glanz (#102115)

From Standards to Success: A Guide for School Leaders Mark O'Shea (#105017)

Future-Focused Leadership: Preparing Schools, Students, and Communities for Tomorrow's Realities Gary Marx (#105009)

Honoring Diverse Teaching Styles: A Guide for Supervisors Edward Pajak (#103012)

How to Thrive as a Teacher Leader John G. Gabriel (#104150)

Leadership for Learning: How to Help Teachers Succeed Carl D. Glickman (#101031)

Literacy Leadership for Grades 5–12 Rosemarye Taylor and Valerie Doyle Collins (#103022)

The New Principal's Fieldbook: Strategies for Success Pam Robbins and Harvey Alvy (#103019)

School Leadership That Works: From Research to Results Robert J. Marzano, Timothy Waters, and Brian A. McNulty (#105125)

Staffing the Principalship: Finding, Coaching, and Mentoring School Leaders Suzette Lovely (#104010)

Teacher Leadership That Strengthens Professional Practice by Charlotte Danielson (#105048)

Teacher Evaluation to Enhance Professional Practice by Charlotte Danielson and Thomas L. McGreal (#100219)

Videotapes

What Works in Schools: School Factors with Robert J. Marzano (Tape 1; # 403048)

What Works in Schools: Teacher Factors with Robert J. Marzano (Tape 2; #403049)

THE WHOLE CHILD The Whole Child Initiative helps schools and communities create learning environments that allow students to be healthy, safe, engaged, supported, and challenged. To learn more about other books and resources that relate to the whole child, visit www.wholechildeducation.org.

For more information: send e-mail to member@ascd.org; call 1-800-933-2723 or 703-578-9600, press 2; send a fax to 703-575-5400; or write to Information Services, ASCD, 1703 N. Beauregard St., Alexandria, VA 22311-1714 USA.